...and then the rains

NUPUR

Woven Words Publishers OPC Pvt. Ltd.

Registered Office:

Vill: Raipur, P.O: Raipur Paschimbar,

Dist: Purba Midnapore, Pin: 721401,

West Bengal, India.

Branch Office(Operations): Hyderabad

 www.wovenwordspublishers.com

Email: publish@wovenwordspublishers.com

First published by Woven Words Publishers OPC Pvt. Ltd., 2020.

Copyright© Nupur Das, 2020

MRP: $20

IMPRINT: WOVEN WORDS RED

ISBN 13: 978-93-88762-16-8

ISBN 10: 93-88762-16-9

Printed and bound by Amazon

To,

All of you who didn't always go protecting your hearts,

Otherwise you would have missed half your life

Tankalia 2019

Beginnings

First in blinded shadows I tread
Timelessly the drops emerged on earth
Journeying as if upon an unseen path
Around a parched and imaged cage
My anklets ached and yearned to dance
In splendour...my feet touched the torrential bliss
captivated by the black witch of my body
pirouetted...in a rich realm of wet arrows
And all the darkness of the cloud
ripped around me like a moonstone robe
The torrents softly besieging my old desire
As if a sigh from some forgotten night
I stood drenched, aloof yet near...my feet swept in Heavenly
trance
Myself forgotten and held captive in the caress
Then out of the engulfing river
I stood bathed in light streaming with eternal hues
The Rain

When you meet someone so different from yourself, you don't have to shake hands to have fireworks go off. It's like Diwali *patakas* in your heart all the time. I always wondered, do opposites really attract? Now I know for sure they do. I had grown up going to the library as often as most people go to the supermarkets. He did not need to read about exciting people or places. He goes out and finds them, if he had time he would do it every evening. The things I like are pretty simple, raw nature, solitude, watching movies, baking cakes and pets. It's like I was a salad with a little vinaigrette and he is a platter of exotic spicy Indian delicacies. A food patriot hands down! Alone we are good. Together we are fantastic.

The reason as to why I am attracted to him is because it gives me a little relief from the burden of being myself. Okay I am not quite but that's okay. I talk non-stop and can put Wikipedia to shame guess to make up for his lack of non-talking.

"You are always saying you are gonna shoot him, why do you keep him around for anyway?" Because he is only one who makes me laugh. Because, I know why, he adores me. Because he needs somebody to look after him and nobody else knows how. Because everything about us is wrong and I never want it to be right.

Because I wake up every morning to his calls, his stupid self and I remember I love him so much I don't know what to do, I love him. I love him. I love him.

"I know what love is, it is because of you"

- Herman Hesse

You journey six hundred plus odd miles to be stranded on a highway, hailing a yellow cab with not much luck, for you have defied the ordinary, as people stare at you from overcrowded buses and pavements gaze at you, you reckon nothingness. You hardly seek any approval; empty introspection is not your cup of tea. The humidity of the city makes you realise that you love mediocrity, cause to you, love cannot be guaranteed in artificiality.

It's in an earthenware pot, a syrupy concoction called love. This thing called life or whatever it is, is short, guess one doesn't have too many visuals in between us but then what we have in between them is, a story of endless laughter. A story of traversing in a yellow cab in a hot summer evening, where a soul provided what life did not magic, in an earthenware pot of a concoction called tea, as the summer moon struck raindrops in the arteries.

How do we know what's right for you? You know the answer. "Follow your heart." The stars are beautiful because of the space in between them just as music is the space in between notes that is where one wants to die and maybe exist too in all this magic.

*B*y the middle of February, it would be time to part from Jakhirpur. Maa used to be busy packing from dawn to night... right from *muri*(puffed rice) tins, *bori, shukno kul*(dried berries), *neem pata*(neem leaves), *holud*(turmeric), *murki*, fine *cheeray*(chiwda), *aahtop chal*, various types of *dal, gota sorshay*(whole mustard), *ghanir* pure oil, *kheer, khajurayer gur*(date tree jaggery), *aahkee gur*(sugarcane jaggery), *taytul*(tamarind), various types of *aahchar*(pickle), practically a little supermarket...I remember the servants busy packing...from days before...tying them in white cloth...it was almost like a ritual...those days there was no cartons.

As the days lengthened ...the fields got dustier and barren...a kind of emptiness all around...days before we left the village... every one of our so called *'prajas'* used to come to meet us and pay homage to *'Boro babur Bou'* and *'Beti'*...bringing along something with them...sometimes even money...and blessing us...I hated all these social customs...all I wanted to do was run wild in the fields and escape for one last time with Nitai.

Thammma would get extra busy...scrubbing me all the more...so that my Father would not complain, I had become dark...having a bath with *kancha-holud*(raw turmeric) would get more vigorous...the night...before we left as the shadows would lengthen over Jakhirpur, Thammma would open her jewellery box, the oil lamp would glow, as she would take out a ring, a piece of ear-ring, or a bangle, and give me a precious piece. ...I hated it all...cause it just didn't attract my childhood mind...not that it even does now.

'Journey along' the teacher said...It would almost take us the whole day. The bus ride from Balurghat to Siliguri would be endless. My father would be awaiting with the office vehicle to take us back to dear Kanchendzonga...and slowly as the jeep would wind its way up home...my head on my father's lap...By then, I would have forgotten the lone forlorn figure draped in a white widow's drape…standing at the main door of our ancestral home…her eyes full of tears hugging me close to her bosom… many years later…when the March breeze gathers up on my dusty balcony…I try to desperately touch Thammma's face…to gather that one diamond like teardrop.

I was in the Cathedral Mont Saint Michael, in the Normandy coast of the south of France, praying desperately for Bucephil. He was barely a month old, and Parvo, the dreaded virus had attacked him. Vets had given up all hope on his survival. He was on saline drips and his frail body was collapsing more with each passing day.

Babua was firmly against Bucephil inhabiting our little flat, and the more he rejected the more adamant Nikkon became in saving Bucephil. When all this was happening back home, I was away in Europe praying fervently in every church and every house of God, that someday soon I would reach my hearthstone, and get a chance to hug Bucephil, close to my heart, even if it meant just once.

Bucephil is my friend in loneliness and solitude. You could be a Priyanka Chopra or Christian Doir, or even a *paanwala* who advertises on television and your dog would think you are the greatest thing ever; at least Bucephil thinks that of me. He is the mirror that reflects my very being. So the very best thing I can do for Bucephil is to remain happy, because Bucephil is happiest in a happy home.

In the beginning of the year I told Nikkon, I am fifty-six, and everything is getting to me. "Then I know what's good for you," Nikkon said in a milder tone. "Do you want another man in your life? Someone who could talk to, two arms around you; a voice from the next room when you're lonesome?"

"I wouldn't mind that, Nikkon. Someone who wouldn't care if I was fat, or had wrinkles, what hardships I have had to overcome, someone who would kiss my tears, and love me regardless of anything."

At the end of a terrible day, I look forward to nothing more than coming home and lying on the bed, under the covers, with Bucephil's sweet whines of happiness, his wet kisses. His unconditional love, simple acts of affection, and the way he cleans the tears from my face. The best part of the day, is sitting with him in the confines of the room, with the Television switched on, both of us oblivious to it. Bucephil is my partner in my crime. My midnight strolls are not complete without him, as both of us bite into forbidden fruits. He gently licks my hand clean of all the melted chocolate. Then he rubs his nose on my night clothes. I know I can buy more clothes, but never another Bucephil.

This home of us is just a thing. It's the heart beats of Bucephil that makes it come alive. Bucephil is a lamb and an angel all in one. So in the New Year get excited about life. Pet your curiosity. Get in touch with your emotions.

Here are 5 ways to make existence worth it all.
1.Detox from the trash box occasionally (I mean television)
2.Stop reading the leftovers (Yes I mean newspaper)
3.Detox from technology in general (WhatsApp, Facebook, Messenger Internet)
4.Walk in nature (if possible) with a pet
5.Come home and meditate.

The universe loves you and so do I.

I didn't have the best of relationships with you...it was more with Baboo. I hated, the way you egged me on with my studies, from my graduations to my post grad and finally to my Ph.D, I simply wanted to flee from it all.

I never liked the way, you taught me to be careful with my finances and not to trust anyone blindly, I just didn't want to believe in you.

I abhorred it when you scolded me for being careless or caught me talking on the landline to guys post-midnight; I simply wanted to run away from home.

I detested the way in which you spoke your mind out at my umpteen mistakes and thought it was the widest generation gap that could ever exist.

I cried myself to sleep, when you didn't buy me a new pair of jeans which I so coveted, or give me extra pocket money to have more fun, I thought you were heartless.

It's been four long years...since you and Baboo have gone...and as I try to stand tall in this game called life...I realise it's too late...to say, that at last, I have found the gems of truth which you so wanted me to have...Love you Maa. I wish I could tell you that for the one last time. For the one last time.

*M*onday morning, and to not hit the Office Circuit, is a luxury, that's rare. Oh! Yes, I have my Krishna to thank for. It's a pleasantly busy mid - afternoon, at home, attending to the chores in the kitchen. Basanti has decided to spend the day wooing Lord Krishna, and I am left, trying out my little triumphs over a fish fry, with YouTube as an ever ready assistant.

The familiarity of the phone ring cuts across the humid sultry afternoon. It's him, explaining to me the nuances of the chain. "It can't be done here," he says, "these chains are machine made, and is only made in Bombay." "Bombay! Don't be funny," I utter, "You must be crazy! The chain is at least more than a century old. Those days, there were no machines to make jewellery, and you tell me it could only be made in Bombay."
"You must be grossly mistaken," I retort back.

Mrinalini, was not pretty by everyday standards, you could almost mistake her for any other woman on the road, but there was something ever so extraordinary about her ordinariness. She was barely ten, when she was married off by Hindu rites, into a zamindar family. Though years older to her, yet her husband loved her dearly...and through him she bore him sons and a daughter, and through them came her grandchildren.

My long winter vacations, would be spent listening tongue tied to her tales of yore and the vision that stays ever so fixed in my soul is of...Mrinalini, clad in a white "than"(six and a half yards of white cloth, worn by widows), no piece of jewellery adorned her, frail self, except for a thin gold chain wrapped around her neck. At rare moments, she would, open her jewellery box, show me a stone studded bangle, a faded jewelled necklace, a splendid earring, each piece so beautiful and so intricate. I would look forward to the days, when she would fervently wish she would do it more often. Sometimes the child in me would seek answers. I wondered and at times, why she never wore them? A pained look, would smear her face...Maa had once told me, Thamma being a widow did not wear jewellery.

The half-done fish fry, implores me to get over with it. Nikkon is hungry. My thoughts leave the fish, and the Master Chef YouTube.

Mrinalini had grown up in a pretty little village by the River Padma. As a child she would roam amongst the paddy fields, free and wild as a bird. Her anklets making music wherever she went, till the day, she was married off, and went to live with my Thakurdada. My Thakurdada had died, long before I was born, and all that I knew of him, was from the photos of a stern looking gentleman, and from what Thamma, told me, a lot like a medieval feudal Lord. Meanwhile other things were happening outside, the tiny world of Mrinalini's. The year was 1947. Jinnah had declared the separate country of Pakistan. The terrible Partition fever was on. Thousands of refugees crossed borders every day, leaving behind their homes and beloved hearth, and all that they had grown to love and treasure. Along with many, Mrinalini too trudged her way, to make a new home for herself in India.

"Buchirani, do you know where Bombai is?" "Why Thamma?" In all my new found knowledge of learning by heart the number of states India had and all the capitals. I would proudly explain.
"It's Bombay Thamma, and not Bombai, and it is the capital of a state called Maharashtra." Thamma would have a faraway look. "How far is it?" she would counter question. I would open my school Atlas and try to explain, that Bombay was far away from Bengal...meanwhile forty-five years had passed. Thamma had long gone, and like some unseen force, almost like a fated discovery, KM mentioned, the chain and strangely. Bombay... "these types of chains are only made in Bombay."

The night was cold and dark. Naseer had to save Mrinalini, and her family. The Hindu family living in a predominantly Muslim area, had planned to leave everything and in the silence of the night flee to India. Naseer was a young lad. Often he would come to my Thakurdada's home, to discuss business, borrow money from him to go to Bombay, for his trade. He dealt in gold jewellery. He would come with his exquisite pieces of jewellery, visit the inner quarters of the household where the ladies resided, to show his collections.

"Maa when have you last seen a movie? Do you want to watch Netflix?" The phone rings, familiar numbers, I just don't want to talk. "Maa do you want a beer?"...I don't want anything... Nothing.

Standing transfixed, I shiver in the afternoon heat. I want to scream to the void in my emotions. I want to tell Mrinalini so much. Above all I want to assure her, "I understand you Thamma...I do. Yes, I do."

"I pray for this Girl, Oh yes! For the young Girl who just landed on Mother Earth! The one about to turn five with a smile or the other one who just turned mine. She is not only mine. My Mother's Grandmother's neighbour or Friend's daughter. She is like a flower very fragile, yet so gorgeous. An Angel whose wings are invisible"

- Gift Gugu Mona- From my Mother's Claverson: badge of Honour for a remarkable woman.

We sat together for a little photo...as always she is shy. Almost like a lost kitten. Little does she realise the lost kitten has a lost mother too. She always remembers to smile for a photo. Last time I had told her, as I repeated again today, whatever the adversaries in life, she should face it with a smile, just like her father does.

I hold on to her, for some more time, we both don't know what to say. She is in awe of me, almost as if to say, I am obliged for everything you do for me, I want to tell her, 'your father has dreams for you,' I want to tell her so much, she does not give me the privilege, I look at her slowly, almost pleading, as she moves away...to those teeming millions of girl children heading to their own perilous directions.

I retrace my steps towards the far away beckoned horizon...and hope she is still smiling.

They asked if I could sleep that night
I said "I do not know"
"For this loss I could not speak
the tongue lay idle in great darkness
the heart was strangely open
the moon had gone
and it was then when I said, "she is no longer there
that the night put its arms around me
and all the white stars turned bitter with grief…"

*I*t always drizzled on the 31st of August...as if the rain Gods wept in solitude.

Maa, used to wake up very early on the 31st August mornings, even before the first ray of light touched the hills atop Dowhill, wherein lay the cremation grounds of Kurseong town. Quietly there used to be a flurry of activity at home. She used to get ready a packet of incense sticks, a candle, a bar of chocolate and a few flowers...lovingly and with utmost care Maa would arrange each and every item with her nimble fingers.

Baboo, used to have his bath, wear something warm, carry his umbrella and in a small bag put in all the things Maa had arranged for Bunu…And slowly he would make his journey, up the hill, towards Dowhill.

With the years Baboo's health deteriorated, but still a lone forlorn figure would walk up all the way to the Dowhill cremation, grounds to be with his two-and-a-half-year-old daughter whom he had lost to cancer.

As I grew older...I used to urge Baboo to hire a car to go up to Dowhill...but he never relented, in spite of all odds in his failing health and the weather, he made his annual pilgrimage to his daughter's last resting place on foot...years gave way to more years...but every year on the 31st of August, a father trudged up the hills to be with his daughter, braving the down pour, his poor health and his age to take her a bar of chocolate which his so daughter loved and sit for a while on the banks of the stream and stain his ears to hear her laughter.

Today Baboo is no more, neither is Maa...and as I write this, I wonder why I didn't ever accompany him? Why did I not even ever ask him...if I could go along with him?...his grief must have been so overwhelming...Yet the beauty of it all is, he missed her, and in his journey up the hill...he must have cherished her "missingness" for in grief he was one with her.

Grief is a great gift...I love the way it keeps my heart soft...I love the way I see it in each of your eyes...as I walk the earth today...It's the hallmark of humanbeingness.

"*M*aa...Now I understand why Dadu (his grandfather; whom he adored) kept silent all the time!!"
"Why Nikko?" I retort.
"Simple Maa, everyone around him were all so basically dumb, that's why he only kept to himself!"
It hit me.
Nikkon will be finally home after seven long months...It's 10.30 in the morning, "What time does your flight reach Bagdogra Nikkon?"
"2.10"
"Entering the capitalist enclave Maa, had ordered a Mayonnaise Chicken sandwich which contains neither Mayonnaise nor is it remotely anything chicken...and it costs 150 bucks!!! Back in the hostel 150 rupees would have seen me through three days of lunch dinners and breakfasts." That was the longest sentence he had spoken in a long time. Monosyllables was all I ever heard.
A momentary silence broken by my hesitant murmuring on the phone, "I should be in the University...Why don't you drop by on your away home?"
"If you say so Maa," yet another moment of silence broken.
Immediately I retort, "It's ok Nikko…"
Post 3 pm it's break at work when I hear a knock on my chamber. I utter … "Come in."
I witness Nikko in all his glory...long hair (I never had a haircut in the last seven months.)
A pair of worn out trousers (in need of immediate washing.)
A 'Tee' which had seen better days...
We hug each other...it's the "now."
That's all that I have...that's all.
Its been one and a half days...my head is full...M Foucault, Albert Camus...basics with C. W. Wills, after months...I start reading some sense...'Catcher in the Rye.'
"Nikko will you go and watch the movie "Tamasha" with me?"
"Maa the last time you had taken me for a movie, it was the worst day of my life!!"

I react immediately.
"Stop reacting Maa!
Start thinking…"
And as I sit and share this with all of you
Comes another retort...
"So you are on Facebook!...Guess you don't have a head that's why you are in it. Will you for a change talk to real people...Good night Maa."
As I write this I am made to understand, we all have had phases, ideologies which have shaped us, and someday we will grow out of it too...
Someday even Nikko will.
I didn't say this...
It's Nikkon who believes in this...as he politely or impolitely deconstructs life's edges...sucking out the very dirt from under his own nails, to remind him from where he came from.

So you left me Bunu! Right beyond my line of sight. You were
the first person who taught me that forever, did not mean
living happily ever after, no Snow White no Cinderella, no happy
endings!

But you taught Maa, Baboo and me, our biggest lesson in our
life, to let go...but none of us ever could. With each passing time
you coloured and inhabited and magnified our unrequited love.
Year after year you made Baboo walk up the road to Dowhill. His
frail health braving the rains and the mists in his eyes, to take a
packet of Nutties, some flowers and incense, to lay at the
crematorium. His journey must have been ever so lonely, yet, he
trudged up, till his body too gave up the steady beat. Every day,
you made Maa light incense sticks, wipe the dust of your photo
frame: a routine engulfing pain, eternal was her love for you till
the day death again emerged. This time it was on her horizon.

So you left me, Bunu, alone to confront the worst in me, in order
to discover the best in me...and you Baboo and Maa have taught
me, to finally count on my fingers the number of sunsets...and I
don't want to miss any of them, cause I have learnt to accept that
one day, I too will die, so I want to make the best out of life and
that's the big secret. That's the miracle.

Nandini Das, died on 31st August of malignant tumor in the
stomach. She was just two and a half years old. I dedicate this
day to all cancer survivors and to all those who have fought
physical and mental pain. It is not easy. Let's appreciate all that
we have built, even if we stand in ruins.

Take care,
Love and hugs.

"The Baronesi: You're far away, where are you? Captain Von Trapp: In a world that's disappearing. I'm afraid."

- The Sound of Music, 1965.

October is a beautiful month to be in Kurseong, a heady mixture of the far away snows, the azure winter line, the marigolds growing wild on the hillside and the glorious festivities enchanting the very saffron air.

On such a day as this, when the blue skies kissed the far away pines, and the sun smiled a bit too often, Baboo and me sat on the steps of our home as he read aloud to me. It was from an extract written by the daughter of a renowned Bengali writer. Since childhood, Baboo had always read aloud to me, especially more so, writings in Bengali understanding my shameful grasp of my mother tongue. When I had finally left home for the outer shores of life, there would be these phone calls "Mamoni there is an excellent article in today's newspaper, please make sometime and go over it." Sometimes he would read aloud on the phone itself. In fact, my brush with history, philosophy, the arts, politics, architecture began with my Father. The nuances of literature, a forgotten poem, an article in The Statesman, a piece of writing in a *Pujosankha*. And every Sunday, it was ritualistic as he would read aloud, his narrations tugging my heart and wanting even more.

That fateful October morning, strangely it was the last time his voice would resonate in hills back home. By November a terrible cerebral attack robbed him of his power of speech. I recollect the afternoon so vividly, as we sat on the steps, crying together with the writer, as she, reminisced about her own father, her growing up days. Baboo's voice was choked as he read and tears rolled down his daughter's eyes, and both their hearts wept in perfect unison. If I could frame one moment for the one last time, it would be this.

The months, post that fateful afternoon, life changed drastically. By May, Maa had bid adieu to us. Pujo was early that year. On Asthami, the Sun dawned clear on the Siliguri sky. In the morning I asked Baboo if he wanted to go home to Kurseong. In sign language he meant a 'No.'

After Maa left had left us, he never wanted ever to go home to Kurseong, maybe the memories were all too stark. But I remember driving him a bit above Sukna, from where the hills could be viewed. He could barely stand on his feet. Yet Baboo, Rita and me, looked up to the Himalayas. I held his feeble hands in mine, and for that one last time I laid my head on his frail shoulder.

Home is where the heart is, our land our Himalayas. But life doesn't take you back the same old way. And just a few months later when the hills once again came alive with the music of the winter sun, the brilliance of the Kanchendzonga, the riot of marigolds and cosmos, Baboo left me too, to join Ma. It was just a matter of five months. And across the hills which we both so adored I still strain my ears every day, for that precious "voice of music."

A wintry evening at Jakhirpur when the shadows on the walls resembled sharks, engulfing the eerie stillness of the air. Far away in the distance the jackals howl, cut across the darkness of the night.

On such a night as this, Thanma wished to go to the shashan. It was not Thamma's sudden fault that she wanted to do so. Her husband had died, and then her brother, and now she wanted to do the same. May be she thought going to the shashan, amidst the barren, the desolate, would absorb her despair.

I told my Mother about Thamma's wish, but Maa said, "No woman in the village goes to the sashan."

Early one morning, as the sun had barely woken from the night long slumber, Nitai, Thamma and me sneaked through the doorway of her home and made our way across the village to the shashan. Thamma walked bare-feet. She always did. She spoke of the death of her husband, as if it was one of those birds, that sits forever on your shoulder. The claws pressed tightly, until there is a blue scar where the claw had perched.

I ask Thamma, why do you want to go to the shashan? Thamma says it's time she reunited with the dead. Like the time, her childhood friend fell in love with someone involved with the Swadeshi andolon, and who had died for freedom. She was heartbroken, just like Thamma's when Thakurda died.

On the way back, she carries some stones from the river bed, tying it in the *anchol* of her white saree...seeking a touch maybe of her first and only love of her life....

She was all of *'misti'* sixteen, married by Hindu rites to a tender soul, ten years older to her and then I found "The Diary."

As a child, I recollect her diligently penning her thoughts in those pages and my curious mind would wonder, as to its contents. She guarded her Diary like an ever-protective mother, demanding her little space be never encroached upon. At times, I attempted to steal through the pages but my shameful knowledge of my mother-tongue made me grapple through the words.

In a dull cold Sunday afternoon in Siliguri, fifty years hence, she comes alive to me once again, and makes me want to put my head on her lap, and give anything to have her fingers running through my hair.

Apprehensively my hands shiver as I anxiously turn the frail, moth eaten pages of the life of "Ila Das" a mother, and a wife and like Alice, I skip back to her wonder years of those days of fun filled picnics, where the mutton never got boiled, the day her daughter's ears were pierced and how much she had cried the day her daughter wrote her first letter to her father. She watched Dev Anand and Suchitra Sen movies along with her husband, the excitement of learning a new recipe, the farewell dinners she organized for her friends and husband's colleagues, the knitting patterns, the Durgo Pujo and little parties she went to her winter vacations at her family home and how she missed her husband the rains in Kurseong, the plants she watered, the grocery list,

Indira Gandhi, the Mohan Bagan East Bengal matches she listened over the radio, pages of seamless threads that connected the sheer happiness of her simple everyday existence.

"The Diary" portrays no secrets, neither does it reflect any literary wonders and as the pages unfold and I still grapple with my knowledge of the language, the faint sunlight outside catches my eye and the lightness of my feet dance along with her thoughts as I come so alive in her simple joys and the abundance of her life and I realise the thing called "home" is parents, the door of which has been forever shut.

*E*very birth date, despite the hectic schedule, erratic moods, haywire situations and an ever ascending age alongside the increase in sugar levels, blood pressures, back pains and the cluster of small wrinkles formed along the outer corner of my eyes while I smile or laugh (that has not affected in any way the intensity and frequency of my laughter, mind you!), I always witness the awakening of my birth date with anything even remotely associated with the word 'birthday.'

Birthdays, were never there in my growing up years, except for the single packet of Cadbury which Maa got to school, awaited with an almost respectful eagerness. That day, of all days, I would feel extra special, like the Sun had come up only for me and the songs of the birds were meant only for my ears. There was no cake, neither was there any new clothes, yet Maa come over to school with that single packet of chocolate would add up to be nothing short of an exhilarating activity. It promised me a break from the mundane. One look and I would be fiercely protective of it. And at the end of the day I would again go off to a yearlong sleep, to be awakened on the next birth date. I still do. And I hope to keep on doing it, till I am some odd 80 (don't want to cross that line), all toothless and silly!

Gratitude galore to all my friends who wished me today...my precious multilayered inheritance, my overpowering identity. You sure made a conscious living connection between what has been, and what is about to be. You gifted me the most beautiful gift my friends. The gift of Maa and memory.

I remember reading "The Fountain Head" by Ayn Rand, back in the first semester of College and over the years the book somehow remained as a First Aid Box. As the year closes on, I reflect back on the span gone, as I recall a phrase of the book that sticks like Band Aid. "I could die for you. But I couldn't and wouldn't live for you."

It has been a year has been a year of trying to live my life and not someone else's, of admiring family, especially the mutual spaces shared. Of not possessing pictures of togetherness to post. Of happily accepting the three men's wishes of not wanting to be photographed. Above all learning to respect each other. Of falling more in love with their weird quirks and understanding the need of mutual appreciation and cooperation.

'Home' spelt Nikkon's umpteen professor friends, endless talks bordering on philosophy, politics, music and the nuances of staying alive, and discovering ale all over again.

Home, was also the arrival of Bucephil and waking up each morning to his kisses, and getting back after a hard day's work never felt so welcoming. Above everything home spelt silent support, and strength from Babua in whatever one did. The highest virtue is to give I guess and I received so much from family, and moving on never felt so beautifully overwhelming.

I am Eros about much in life. Raw nature. Bygone, unrecalled towns and hamlets. Cobbled dark alley ways, wild flowers that drench the hills. The incessant rains, on tin roofs and window panes, The Kanchendzonga, Soul stirring dusky ragas and of course words. But pens, never. Yet, many a time I did toy with the urge, and dreamt of a day when I would pin a pen on a shirt pocket and head to office, Like my father did, like my better half does. But it was just something to be pushed at the backyards of my imaginations. Till today, when the pen looked imploring at me, all metal classy and bearing a brand (I am more used to its 'plastic' cousins) to be held and used, almost pleading.

Quickly I rummaged through my irrational cupboard for a shirt with a pocket, and then I did exactly what my father did pinned the pen on the pocket. Only Maa was not around to do the honors, to lovingly pin it for me, as she did every day, ever so proudly for my father.

Anthony Bourdain

*T*he 'Idiot box' has never quite been my preferred cup of brew, though occasionally I do view a few news channels and often Anthony Bourdain had featured in many. The softer escapist in me nevertheless strayed far from his raw presentations on travel, food and life. Anthony Bourdain did not excite the die hard romantic in me.

Today on a mid afternoon Sunday, with the sweltering heat tearing across the plains of northern India, the television features to the reasons of his suicide, at the age of 61. Nothing deterred him to take his life as he hanged himself with the belt of his hotel bathrobe, not even the adorable faces of his 11 year old only daughter, and his 83 year old Mother.

Bourdain was a Television Hero exploring the truth through food and his fearless travel. As a young man, he beat the harsh hours of being a chef, he beat the drugs he took, heroine, cocaine. He had made a life for himself, earning billions, inspiring millions. A larger than life figure, a gifted chef and a subaltern story teller who used his books and shows to explore, culture cuisine and the human conditions. He advocated for the marginalised populations of the world, and campaigned for safer working conditions for Restaurant chefs, he supported women's rights, immigration issues and is revered by the ordinary people worldwide.

Despite all his strength and honesty depression slowly tickled in and won. Depressions can be invisible, but it can be most powerful deadly and lethal. It exists in many, and even more in people who lead successful and beautiful lives. It just shows how formidable depressions can be.

So love and celebrate all. You never know your actions or words may be the cause of depression for someone, specially for people who are prone to being extra sensitive or more emotional. Some say to be happy you should not be too concerned with others. Consequently there is no escape from it. So the question is "Should I kill myself or have a cup of coffee." (Albert Camus)

At the end I guess one needs more courage to live than to kill oneself. Strangely Bourdain was shooting for the famous Television Series "Parts Unknown." Suciders don't talk...they act.

"Feet, what do I need you for when I have wings to fly?
- Frida Kahlo

*M*anifestations of affections and love are so venerated, be it a hug or a chocolate, a message on social media, a few hieroglyphs on an old bygone Birthday Card or as innumerable times a book. When one was gifted the autobiographical "The Diary of Frida Kahlo" one never yearned to learn a language so hopelessly as one sought to learn Spanish. (Like long ago, one had yearned to learn French, solely to pronounce the names of wines.) An undecipherable desperate madness had gripped the senses as one turned page after page, to decipher Frida's pain, her agonies, her nightmares, her vibrant emptiness, her revolutionary horrors, and above all her intense and fierce passion for Diego...which almost bordered on the powerful.

Mexican-born Frida, suffered from polio as a child, and nearly died of a bus accident. She suffered multiple fractures of her spine, collarbone and ribs, a shattered pelvis, broken foot and dislocated shoulder, and as she lay in a cast in the hospital bed, she took passionately to painting, her physical and emotional pain depicted starkly on her self-portrait. She had thirty surgeries in her life.

Frida's emotional and physical pain is almost iconic. Diego was a womanizer, having multiple liaisons, even having an affair with Frida's younger sister Christiana. Betrayed time and again, rejected often, Frida turned to painting self-portraits. "I paint self-portraits because I am so often alone, because I am the person I know best". "I tried to drown my sorrows, but the bastards learned how to swim, and now I am overwhelmed by this decent and good feeling." A woman who took to Marxist ideologies, and lived most part of her life in her bed in the beautiful *la Kasa Azul* a.k.a the Blue House. Frida, loved her father, more than she ever loved her mother and her dogs were her constant companions.

When Nikkon was three and a half years old one had received a Mexican Government Scholarship to do a Ph.D programme at the University of Mexico, which later one had declined as the thought of leaving one's infant son back home was unthinkable. But there was another clause too to the scholarship, that one had also to learn Spanish. Twenty years later, as one rummaged through the certificates for one's Career Advancement Scheme at the University, the eyes fell upon the letter from the Ministry of Human Resource, Government of India regarding the Mexican Government Scholarship. The tryst with Frida, and her Blue House never occurred nor did the Spanish, but yes, like her the love for one's father more than a mother. The love for dogs, taking to the bed like second skin, and having deep regards for Marx's thought processes and oh yes! Lastly comes love… "Wordless, infinite you" (Frida Kalho.)

*"If I really think that I'm the greatest thing since sliced bread,
it's probably because I've never eaten the sandwich"*

- Craig D. Lounsbrough

Tatyul Pukur,
Late in the afternoon sun…

Most times she short circuits her brain and takes umpteen
liberties with her eyes…
tears and tears and more tears
When it starts there, there are no commas or semi colons neither
can you take a break or drift off for a much-needed snack.

Antonym is N's best friend
Dr. Jekyll and Mrs Hyde…
could be lazing around on a tattered couch shelling sweet
potatoes,
giving you the sweetest smiles.

I was fooled once….
not any more
"I rather not be decoded" declares N
"do you think
I need a shrink?"

I tell her "noooooooooooooo"
For me my darling N
You are a simple story
"once upon a time"
won't really rhyme
you see
I still love you
So, what if you are a
Narcissus enough
to be such a fool."

"The best way to cheer yourself is to try to cheer someone else up"

Love you Zindagi…

A Sunday, where you slyly offer Bucephil two scoops of butter-scotch ice cream, and get caught red handed by Nikkon, and you wonder whether you are once again back in sister superior's office…two bars of ice cream which a friend had lovingly carried along for a lunch meet of sorts…but then Bucephil puts his furry paw in mine and I swear, I want to write a love poem.

A sunday morning, where a soul drops in with yummy Rosogollas, a bottle of red wine and a bouquet of red roses…and you feel pampered and loved. She says it's her daughter's birthday today…and why does it feel as if it's yours.

A Sunday afternoon where you come across a song…and you want to reach out to the mountains, and to school days and you can't wait to share it with all your soul friends…and then a soul friend tags you with your favourite piece of music…It feels like you have camped right in the warmth of a soul.

Yes, a sunday where a daughter sends you a poem by Trista Mateer…and then you sit up and feel privileged that there is some kid who still wants to reach out to you…and yes, something more, there is someone who still needs you.

A sunday, where a friend excitedly remarks of more better business prospects and you wonder…how crazy does that sound, and suddenly you feel less greedy, less needy.
Finally now, something is sinking in and you do not care for it.

Got back physically and mentally drained to the perimeters of the abode. Usually I don't sit back to scribble, immediately on reaching. One rather prefers sleeping it off, the 'tiredness' but, scribble- I had to.

In the samsan there was this frail looking plant, in need of comfort and care and lots of love. It was, lying abandoned and in need of support to grow. One resorted to looking around for some leftover sticks, lying scattered after the dead are set to flames, in order to make some kind of support, for the withering plant. It all felt so good. Gokul looked around for some thread to tie and make frame of the sticks, so that the plant could survive within some fence around it. As one tried the thread around to construct a makeshift framework, it dawned that one's own life was so similar to that of the little plant. Likewise, we, simple mortals need to remain within borders in order to become disciplined and happy in our existences.

I open a message send by a young student where she talks about her father, being her greatest source of strength, and when his physical presence is lacking, God sends others for her in different guises to provide strength. She mentions they are her boundaries, and there is nothing beyond them. She talks of Rousseau, where he says, "Man is born free but everywhere in chains." Further she claims that chains keep grounded. Chains keep one within boundaries, helps one to grow, to achieve one's goal and contributes to humbleness. Finally she adds "I rather live chained forever and never lose sight of boundaries.

"This is my child, I planted it. I saw it grow. I love it. Don't cut it down…"

- R.K. Narayan, Malgudi days.

*I*n Jakhirpur during the long winters, I used to bury my head deep inside the soft tenderness of the quilts. Thammma used to tell me to just stay put in bed, but then Nitai used to come, and together we ran wild in the fields, tending to the umpteen cows. My cheeks would go all red during the winter months.

I remember trying to brush my teeth the way Nitai did, with a neem twig, and how Nitai used to laugh his heart out. At times, together with Nitai we used to wait below the Palm tree, for a glassful of the early morning fresh Palm juice.

The taste of the juice still lingers on my palate, like the only drink I have ever drunk. Nitai knew which trees bore the sweetest berries, in which pond grew the pink lotuses. He knew the names of almost all the trees, and recognised the birds by their twittering. Nitai taught me how to climb trees, to walk barefoot without stumbling, to drink water by folding one's palms. Together we tasted the sweetest tamarind, dug deep into the soft earth for baby potatoes, and went looking for fresh eggs amongst haystacks. He whispered to the fishes, and even swam like them. Nitai was my first buddy and above all, my first Teacher.

I recollect too, the breakfasts Thammma used to make, warm and delicious, consisting of fresh milk, hard boiled eggs [something which Enid Blyton made it sound like the most delicious food ever tasted] and syrupy palm syrup with soft *rotis* made of rice flour, warm from the oven. She used to feed me lovingly with her hands, and then my Sanskrit teacher used to come, to teach me the Mantras. The Surya Mantra, the Gaytri Mantra and the other Mantras. I hated it; all I wanted to do was run with Nitai, with the wind against my hair, my blank feet touching the morning dew, and 'sunshine on my shoulders.'

*B*eginning!

Because all journeys are not happy. May yours be one.
One had the good fortune to meet Father Don Piero at our frugal Chalsa home. It was a warm winter afternoon, as we shared a meal with the priest from Torino along with my friend Patrizia, Renato her husband and Father Cherian. Thirteen years from today to be exact.

Before my Italian sauntering perfected, one wished to be at his grave, nestled in the small beautiful village of Susa on the Italian side of the Alps. The Man who has given much to ones' fellow Indians. And what an end to a beginning!

Notwithstanding one can't wait to reach home. Backpacking much reminiscences of a lifetime. Millions of photographic memories of the sea, the mountains. The gifts of life and the love, that one had received. No bright lights had lured. Nor did the shops turn magnetic as one embarked through the crossings of life. A peripatetic. It was sheer tendrils of love. The smell of the sea. The fresh bread and cheese, The sweetness of the water from the Mountain springs that had quenched one's soul on an autumnal afternoon atop the Alps. The fiery red of the Maple matching the heart yet home beckons. Can't wait to meet Bucephil Babua and Nikkon and Basanti, Uddesh and Narayan. All that spells the sweetness, and security of hearth. Without whom one's journey would have just withered. The simple little things yet profound, in its utter content. Sometimes a beginning is always mistaken for an end.

"At a certain level of suffering or injustice no one can do anything for anyone. Pain is Solitary"

- Albert Camus

*I*t was the spring of 1917. In Montparnasse, the lavender flowers bloomed in wild abundance, overflowing from the Parisian balconies. Jeanne Hèbuterne was crazily in love with the artist Amedeo Modigialini. She did not care whether Modgialini was an alcoholic or a drug addict. She took pride that even though the rest of the world may disagree; she still believed that her love was beautiful.

With months Modigialini's intake of drugs and alcohol escalated, and finally drove him to tuberculosis. Few of his acquaintances knew of his condition. In the 1900s tuberculosis was a dreaded disease, in France and a major cause of death. A horrible sickness and those who had it were feared, ostracised and pitied.

Jeanne, was Modigialini's Muse, amazingly beautiful, delicate and as fragile, as a crystal vase. Her long dark hair cascaded through her back, like luminous clouds on the dark Paris horizon. In the fall of 1918 the couple, moved to the warmer climate of Nice. Modigialini's agent hoped to sell some of his art work to the wealthy tourists who wintered there. But luck barely prevailed. Yet the couple accepted the risk, for them the present meant accepting the risk of future.

On 24th January, on a cold wintry morning, and in the arms of his Muse, Amedeo Modigialini lost his life to tuberculosis. Jeanne was dragged home by her family. She was completely heartbroken, and in acute grief. The next day on 25th January, she walked backwards and threw herself out of the fifth floor apartment window, a day after Modigialini's death, killing herself and her nearly full term unborn child.

It was nearly after ten years, after she took her own life that Jeanne's family had long relented and allowed her remains to be transferred to Père Lachaise Cemetery to rest beside Modigialini. Her epitaph reads
"Devoted companion to the extreme sacrifice."

Tragedy and sadness is a part of life. Some say both of them had disturbed minds. To me the desperate agony of absence like beauty is the person or the beholder's prerogative, and coming to terms with absence can be extremely painful. May be someday I would love to go back to Paris again and visit Père Lachaise Cemetery.

Would you like to join?

The Journey Of The Gypsy Girl's Tambourine
- Doel Biswas

Sometimes dreams come true, in the strangest way, and sometimes, they remain a blur in the long forgotten mists that hugs the hills back home.

I don't know where it all it began, ten years my junior in school, misconceptions about each other that bordered on imposed distances, we barely spoke, leave alone correlate, but then life sets destinies and paths...two people so different yet shaped to come together to face a world with a familiarity of their own depths, their own discovered vulnerabilities...

And like her splendid impromptu speeches, she breathed life into the photos...and strangely the blurs and the boundaries fell miraculously into structures that spoke of beauties in symmetries and touching asymmetries.

And so I took to Amazon, but then Amazon refused to deliver neither at my hearth, nor at office, so off I travelled to seek another Geography, as much as I wanted the moment to be framed, yet the Gypsy girl remained unrequited...so it was the ultimate let go, making the most difficult sacrifice of all, giving away the very thing we want to hold forever...

So neither the autograph nor the frame did happen...as we both entered into another day of sometimes joyful, more often difficult helplessness.

With Rebs the journey is almost subaltern, if not Marxist in it's approach, so when both of us decided to meet in Kolkata, I was prepared for the fascinating if not an extremely charming travelogue, with my dearest friend.

So in the Oxford Book Store in Park Street holding warm memories of her college days and my days of browsing with tea and books, Rebs and me sat through an absorbing presentation and discussion of the true story of Queen Victoria and Abdul her closest confidant by the writer Sharbani Basu, now a brilliant motion picture.

So the city which houses the Queen's greatest Memorial, I sat through a gripping discussion of the 68 year old Queen and her dearest Munshi 24 year old Abdul, a tale of intimacy and tenderness that the British Establishment had tried their hardest to destroy evidence of it.

With Rebecca my paths have always bordered on, shared passions of the extraordinarily ordinary as together we hit the City of Joy, hugs my friend for everything.

*I*t was two years since I had last bid adieu to Audrey on the slopes of Zuluk. We had promised to soul share more often, but then the corridors of time took us on different routes, and all that we were left clutching were memories of another day.

We had tried, desperately to hug the Earth, in Delhi, Pune, Mumbai, Goa, Jaisalmer, Kurseong, Kathmandu...but nothingness had coloured us blue, until the 'City of Joy' becokned. She was enroute to Port Blair, I had lied to my Boss, I had to see her.

Friendship does strange things, as together we breathed in the Durga, the red bordered saree, which belonged to Ma, the silver tea tray, she imagined I would use, we heard our echoes across the age old faded courtyards, and the nolen gurayer mistis played havoc with our pallets...yes we decided to live, to clutch on to the wind, the water and yes the storm.

Kolkata Airport is crowded, like its traffic cluttered streets. The memory of our last night conversations, colours the early morn, as the city wakes up once again. In the cold of the winter air, I hear her familiar laughter singing from the same sunlight before she left, still flowing with me...Audrey Hepburn the light in your eyes come alive again to another future...Till we reappear again, hugs and much love.

So, there is pathetic me, butchered and battered. These days it's bad, even Bucephil keeps away from me, as if I was pest control.

And so there was him…"*awenayk khon kichhu laykho nee keyno?*"…hmm, and so I go all sick of a different variety…more of the love sick variety and churn out one of those narcissist poems for him… (I mean it's tough you know getting narcissistic for others…BJP (the new concept of God) help me!…and help comes packed ever so pathetically…I write one of those poems painting him adorable lovable admirable…and well, much to my lopsided humor…he says, he looked at it once (must have thought it to be some prescription for AIDS) and then its "The End"…literature literally languishing. My brain tells me…"Nupur go for it…the fight"…but then…I have taken, a vow…to go the Gandhi way…non violence (inwardly I swear to myself…no more reactions, from now on just detractions stupid!)

And then finally the phone rings…it's him. I jump upside down…maybe he wants to change tactics, and not just "look" through the poem but "see" it through…haha! how right I am… "*kee koro?*"..I say something stupid, cause Gandhi is glaring at me, from above…"*Jachee!!*" says he. The phone and me both snap…I imagine a Buckingham palace guard taking me by the neck and telling me in absolute polished Oxfordian English… "Get out!"

I wake up to a grayish Friday morning. Uddesh tells me, today, Bucephil has done a two kilometer circuit. Now Bucephil has two more friends to run with him. One of them works in the local bank. He has even bought a folding stick to scare away stray dogs on the road...

I have much to do, clean the home for one...but all that I want to do is write, and play with Bucephil. It has been poignantly beautiful...the few days of being alone with him, as Amrita mentions, at times minimum human contact is essential.

Yesterday night I had this long forgotten need to be tucked in bed, like childhood days...I recollect Baboo doing it all his life, coming to check on me at night...at times, pulling the covers over me, switching off the bedside lamp, keeping aside the book I was reading...and running his hand over my forehead. He would do it more so after Nikkon was born. Every night he would come to check on Nikkon, whether his nappy was dry, pat him to sleep. At times he would be sleep on the carpet, to keep an eye on his grandson.

Many years later, I remember the night I stayed back with Di, in Delhi. Early morning she was at my bedside, putting her caring hand on my forehead, transporting me to my childhood days. A comfort so sought at times. With Nikkon, I would sometimes go over to tuck him...but then, by the time he was living with me... he was a big boy, and Maa was someone he was just staying with...full stop. Sometimes at night I have this deep urge to check up on Bucephil, I tiptoe to Nikkon's bedroom...and there Bucephil would be wagging his tail...we would hug each other, in the quite of the night, it is so comforting.

So I slowly learn to fill some space in my own void. "Nupur, you should learn not to rely on another person, to make you whole.

That life is dangerous"…so I live a little more…and I know,
waiting for the perfect conditions is too far fetched.

Alone I can be just as wide and vast and spellbinding, as any sky
full of stars. someday the world will stop for me…
I know and so does Bucephil.

My first memory of her is something I rather not remember where I left her high and dry at Bagdogra Airport. But the relationship we grew into over the days was too trivial for such memories. Months flew into years and so did our hearts. Her Mother and Aunts are very close friends of mine and she is like a daughter. Over the days she would be diligently there supportive of my all posts, I loved the way she looked at life, her travels, and her family and then we met again.

This time at home in our beloved Kurseong. I caught up with this beautiful young pretty vivacious girl, full of fun laughter and so very full of life and in the process of doing so, I admired what she was wearing.

Her parcel had reached me yesterday and what a pleasure it was to behold in my aged hands, gifts from a daughter, leather sling bag (an overwhelming surprise) and the poncho that I had so coveted. Giving is like an art form, it has to be practiced to be done well and Megs did it all so brilliantly for me. Gratitude is not necessarily something that is shown after an event it is something deeper it is the millions of things that come together love you Meghs for the beautiful girl you have grown up to be. It's indeed a privilege and a pleasure.

Blessings sweetheart

Gratitudes in abundance to dearest Dolly, Mums and Babs.

Ever since Babua's brutal journey with cancer began, life has never been the same for me or all for those who have been close to us inclusive of Bucephil. Cancer is like an Indian marriage, it's like marrying into the whole family. The initial shock was earth shattering. What took over was acute fear, disillusionment, and then "why us" including the ruthless mental and physical toll that Babua himself underwent. It impacted every aspect of our lives.

And with each passing day it was getting impossible to hold up. And slowly I was losing it all. Both Babua and Nikkon kept turning to me every minute, for support, while inwardly I cringed and crumbled.

In the beginning the desperation to be brave or strong was something I chose to just withstand within the boundaries of the family and self, and then one morning, I realised I couldn't carry on with the charade any longer. And so began another journey, the journey of reaching out, of sharing my fear and pain with few, for some I took to the phone, for others at a faraway distance or another continent, I resorted to the messenger and WhatsApp. Some got back, some just left a few words, and some I gather were too busy to bother. But for most, we were held close, hugged with messages of hope, care, prayers, healing lights, added to all this was their very own personal visits to temples churches, monasteries. Masses were held, pujas performed and chants organized in monasteries. Every day without fail, many got back. Some with important information, links, videos, suggestions of healing. Many resorted to video calls, Some came home with healthy cooked food, most times on a regular basis. Help came in different forms and variations loaning mixer grinders, food processors, gifting plants, books, providing us transportation, on a daily basis. Some stood with us, relentlessly for days during our endless waits at the hospital, even helped trim Babua's beard. And practically, the whole world was at our doorstep. Many travelled miles, took flights. A youth who helps me with keeping my home clean, bought a ticket on a train, in an ordinary sleeper class and practically walked from the railway station at Kolkata to reach us. As if slowly and steadfastly a miracle was occurring in our very own lives. What had initially devastated our little world started to heal. Love, faith, hope, strength and positivism took over. Initially it took a lot of adjusting. One had to be strong, at least **pretend to be** as stress free as one could ...and I don't think each of us would ever achieved that. Had it not been for all of you...you gifted us miracles.

Among the many videos, ranging from cures, to words of courage to medical jargon that friends had shared, one was a TED talk entitled. "What dying taught me about living" where a young girl, affected by Leukemia speaks of her journey with cancer and the blog she had started. Towards the end of the video she talks about undertaking an epic journey, post survival to try and meet all those souls who had contributed ever so encouragingly to her recovery. The video kind of got into me, and I discussed the idea, with Babua to embark on a pilgrimage too, and convey our heartfelt gratitude, in person. Trying to be acutely aware, of paying our own heartfelt attention to each of you. So here begins my little pilgrimage. I began my journey with my office, beginning at the University of North Bengal. Next stop Bengaluru...

Someday God willing I hope to journey to each of your homes...

*S*till, even during mundane Monday mornings, in a small clumsy town, such as this, and even in the much needed solitude and shared traumas of the months gone by, and the humid weeks between summer and autumn, I feel kind of satiated as I take to the wee bit of the veranda at home with Bucephil. The sporadic, torrential downpours hit the earth, as I sit wrapped in a shawl, (which I suspect, is actually a cotton table cloth)...I listen to birdsongs and surrender myself to the raw and simple intricacies of life. Bucephil joins in the calmness and satisfaction of my existence. Far, far away a friend hits the metro early morning and sends a photo.

I tell her "You look like a drug addict." She smiles, she has partied all night and slept at four in the morn, in her friend's tee shirt, cause she says, nothing else fit her.

I resonate with her joy in thinking the same thoughts, feeling the same feelings...making the world more real, I guess. On WhatsApp, a photo of a magazine cover of a friend, who has been a cancer survivor catches my eye…my curiosity soars and I want details. "It's meant to be a surprise" my other friend says...a gift of a magazine, sent from another corner of the world, by a friend, where, some words of mine had accompanied her arduous journey. I rejoin my other friend. "I want to talk" I say. Her answer comes all raw, all me. "I am doing the *jharoo*" (the monosyllable which literally means "brooming") My thoughts take a merry go round, just like the pouring rain. She promises to get back, once she is through. These are all promises of love, of faithfulness. Of shared evenings and doggy tales. Promises of talking late into the night, and waking up mid afternoon as the sunlight pours through the white linen curtains, and into our souls. So Monday morning filters through the warm cup of brew, and I realise that life, someday, will break us. I also realise that we will rise again tomorrow. And together rise the day after that. Until our feet painlessly touch the ground beneath us and the smiles on our faces reach our souls. And I can tell myself, indeed, blessed I am with the truest of friends...

*I*t's mid-morning, and the Android beeps. I immediately make a beeline for the other line...the 'lifeline.' He smiles ever so sexily at me from technology. It warms my soul and makes me want to turn around, walk out of the door, and find a dance floor to hit.
I didn't except the call, leave alone yap for so long a stretch. "You okay na?" my friend asks.
"What?"
I get struck by lightning.
"You know what I was pained by your tears yesterday."
So here it comes finally the unabridged version.
I reply… "Yes a bit messy but yes I am good."
I don't tell the person, I wanted to do cartwheels in spite of my Osteoarthritis. And that I had seen the tears in my friend's eyes.

We jabber endlessly. My friend tells me bits and pieces about the story that one is reading. It is good to listen to for a change. Basically my friend's brain cells sinks into an area of his body that makes the person shut up the moment I open my mouth. But today is an exception. A dictionary defines Soul Mate as: A person who is perfectly suited to another in temperament. Before I met my friend I was mad.

My friend fits me without a flaw. At the beginning my friend must have been apprehensive that I might swallow the person whole and my friend might disappear for having me. After the time spent together I am certain that my friend understands the person is the night to my day. And we both have the same philosophy, value, control, individuality and independency. No one disappears. We are like an equinox. Just like the day moves into the night and then night into day, we both complete each other and build a partnership. We are two different entities, co - existing superbly, letting each other be but never leaving each other's side.

This was now officially the most sensible conversation we have had in a while...and that included a debate on the lengths we could go for each other.

Most of the times my friend begs to differ. "What do you say?" I ask "You think you are the only one that can jump off a cliff for me!" "Even I can"...I paused, listened, took the god damn Android as close as I could, to hear him speak and figured, yes our temperaments were indeed similar...mad.

Sunshine on my shoulders; sunshine in my soul and sunshine in my heart.

The month of April has always been ever so beautiful, dollops of sunshine, spring in the air and the vivid hues of flowers that bloom in gay abandon....and sunshine's waves of laughter.... evanescent music to my weary ears. She loads me with money, she always does, heaps of it, "I want you to buy a smart overcoat or a warm jacket for your trip to Europe" she says. I do neither. A year gone by, I take out the off shoulder I had picked up with her money...I miss her. It has been long since I last met her...so much has happened, as I try to pick up her loving threads and weave them into rays.

I try to recollect my first encounter with Sunshine...resplendent in a beautiful saree, her presence filling the Salt Lake City Centre with asymmetries and symmetries of beauty. Sunshine is an inner and outer complexion living in one face. Beauty specially occurs in the meeting of the time with the timeless, her tireless caring of me during my operation, her spiraling dance steps, her sense of holding on to bonds, however rough or smooth, her sexy eyes in the failing evening light, her wonderous cooking and the magic of her laughter, ringing past the sultry night air.

She is my incredible comfort zone, tough yet strikingly beautiful in her own vulnerabilities. She is sunshine amongst the pine trees of winter and the Krishnachuras of summer, and that sweet pang right before you gorge on your favourite desert : you know you're in for it.

I am so in for it.

*B*abs, was her usual overflowing self...all Home, Helenite and Hills, with help for hotels, weather, clothes, transport...you just had to name it she would be there, for everything I needed, making time from her busy schedule…

"Nups the phone just got disconnected maybe because you were travelling back, anyway, safe travels...so come home directly so that we can spend more time I would have come to the airport to receive you all but then I need to cook dinner before you reach. Dolly Di called me today she will try her best to come, otherwise, you and I both shall decide when to go to see her on Monday...Just finished doing dessert strawberry cheesecake and brownies with hand churned coffee ice cream have lunch and board after that do not eat any outside food am making done snacks to munch…"

Overwhelming in their passions are Babs and Bhai (Gopal flying down, just a day back from Canada) with their 'antorikota'...and as the September rain cradled their beautiful garden, and we sipped our wines...I wished I could relive the day over and over again, not to change things, just to recreate all the magic a million times.

And so I trudged up to the 12th floor of Oakwood Residency, drunk on the last drop of French Afertif, and Babs and Bhai felt much more than a treasured possession...they felt home.

*T*owards the end of my journey, I realized I had no photographic memory of my friend. Maybe, the need was just not there...so finally I turned to Renato, her dear husband...atop the Mountains, at Mueini and that is all I have. The rest is in my soul, which she has been a part of for more than fifteen years.

We Indians pride ourselves on treating our guests well...I don't want to sound bitter, but instances have happened with many of us in life, where one has succumbed to pain or humiliation at someone's home. Patrizia is not someone I meet everyday or talk too, regularly, she owes me nothing yet for twenty or more days, she made me feel ever so precious, at home, and above all respected.

The Lady who for the last fifteen years, has stood every Sunday, in front of a church in her native Italy with a begging bowl, along with her husband begging for money for the poor of my country. At times, the Parish priests have been not so welcoming. Many a times, the people coming to the church have not been forthcoming. Some have made snide comments about India being a developing country and why should they need donations? Yet, hail rain or storm she stood every Sunday, in front of a church begging for money. And she has been doing this, not for a few Sundays or a few months or years, but for the last fifteen years...

The first Sunday, that I was there, I was blessed to witness it all, and I could see the tears of joy in her face as they collected 1947 Euros.

Many of you have heard about Jesu Ashram in Siliguri. She has helped build a leprosy hospital there, and Jesu Ashram is what she breathes. She has helped provide mid day meals in many closed Tea Gardens in the Duars, have come up with a school for the poor in Mongpu(Darjeeling) with the collaboration of the Darjeeling Jesuits, and she was saddened about the grandeur of

North Point School Darjeeling, in contrast to the terrible condition of a school run by the very same Jesuits at Mongpu. She has helped in providing drinking water in the Kolkata Bhagar, and in many areas in and around Krishnagar. She breathes and lives the Indian poor and all this she has been doing in utter silence...for the last so many years, from the day she first step foot in our country.

Become with every breath, the Incredible creature you wish to be (so untrue to this thought I have been) the most remarkable thought about human existence is how often we are allowed to press the 'restart' button and how little we actually use it.
I present to you, my friend, Patrizia Bianconi.

I dig the way she survives. Survival looks so gorgeous on her. You see no marks below Gypsy's eyes, maybe deep inside, but I loved the way she looked right through them and laughed that sexy laugh of hers. You know what; even life was quite taken aback at her spirit and me. I was like...that's The Girl!!! And friends, she did all of this with so much of style, élan, and grace...gosh! Born model that she was. She walked through the ramp of glass and over fire. I recollect that message of hers, that fateful winter morning.

"Hey Nups, you know what I am diagnosed with cancer."
I am not interested in people who haven't lived or died a few times; who haven't yet had their heart ripped out, or know what it feels like to lose everything. I knew what she has been through. I admire the pride she has in her vulnerability! That's her.

Gypsy is like a butterfly whose wings have been touched, yet she flies high. Whether something was meant to be, or meant to leave, did not matter to her anymore. She soaked up the sun, kissed the breeze and she flies today regardless of going in for her chemotherapy again tomorrow, a girl with an unwritten story, leaving a lasting impression like a lipstick smudge on a soft tissue. I dedicate the "Cancer Survival day" to my dearest friend "Gypsy."

'Memory's images, once they are fixed in words are erased', Polo said. 'Perhaps I am afraid of losing Trieste all at once, if I speak of it, or perhaps, speaking of other cities, I have already lost it, little by little'

Invisible Cities
Italo Calvino

The night in Venice was enchanting. Patrizia and me matched our steps with many that swarmed Piazza San Marco while in the distance, the gold on the wings of the Angel atop the bell tower, flashed. One stood amongst hundreds of people, yet alone. did I miss anyone? Strangely one did not. Last time round Venice was like a raw wound...bleeding. This time the wound had been bandaged with love and care. May be the optimism was derived from the haze of cathedrals that greets you at every bend. And like Istanbul the pigeons and seagulls provided the much needed company.

If you happen to wake up in Venice, specially on a Sunday, the music of innumerable bells, surges forth like the most melodious wake up calls one has ever heard. You feel as if you are in a temple town back home. The beauty of Dodge's Palace, a stark contrast to the melodrama that Venice offers. Venice is kind of understated I feel, it's architecture less valued. The primary focus being romance. Those school girl days of my English Literature class takes precedence. The merchant of Venice.

'Lorenzo; in such a night did Jessica steal from the wealthy Jew, and with an unthrift love did run from Venice, as far as Belmont.'

Patrizia's shutters work randomly. I lean against the bridge's marble balustrade, and as I look far down the darkening canal, my psychology takes a nosedive....Venice is so fragile yet so grand and resilient....
I wake up wanting to be a bit like Venice.

I enter the chaotic confines of Bagdogra Airport, leaving behind home and hearth on the afternoon of the festival of lights en-route to the capital. A bit disoriented and apprehensive.

In Bagdogra I meet a younger colleague who too is travelling to the same destination along with his wife, a Breast Cancer patient, she is heading to the capital for an operation...and it dawns there is so much in life not to complain about. I travel Air India the Government carrier, and enjoy the leg space and reach Delhi, half an hour early before schedule.

The terminal at Delhi drills into my head that yes, I am into the city which thrives on distances. So I lug my bag, try not to crib about my walk and head toward the luggage belt. Technology comes to the rescue as I hop on to the lift, and I share the space with a young girl. I smile at her. Come on! It is Diwali. No return smile, instead an arrogant disdain. It kind of hits me… "I have entered the inhospitable Metro."

At the arrival, lounge, my adorable junior is there. We catch up. She is sparkling and is overjoyed to see me...tells me I am looking nice and wants to take a selfie...the goodness of shared bonds cuts across all dark thoughts and nothing is lost...suddenly everything is sparkling.

It's 11.30 Indian Standard Time...as I walk into Milano Malpensa. The journey from home to another home has been slightly tumultuous. As I window shop at Delhi Duty Free, I cannot help but indulge in some extravaganzas, as I buy myself some Chanel war paints and a perfume from Burberry for a dear friend. Meanwhile I wonder why there are no pet shops at Duty Frees, don't people feel the need to carry home something for their pets. I miss Bucephil ever so much.

Meanwhile on board Air India, air sickness hits me like wild fire, but then I am at home, as the Air India Crew are more than concerned, and so are my co passengers. The humble Eno comes to my rescue so does my flight mates, ordinary Indians...but then, I am glad I took an Air India flight.

At Milano, Patrizia and Renato are more than welcoming, they are all love and care. My heavy suitcase is lugged, my bags are taken care of, I am given a choice of warm pullovers to wear…

Assuming that I have travelled from a warmer climate...and I am escorted to the front seat to sit beside Renato, as Patrizia takes to the back, for a two hour drive to Torino. On the way, we touch base with a roadside Restaurant, and it's time to fall in love with the grilled salmon and green peppers all over again.. My sweet tooth bites on to the gelato. Finally the car sails through the Italian night air...my destinations beckon.

Early morning I take a walk in the park, just outside Patrizia's home...and soak in the European autumnal colors…it's peaceful as I try not to miss all my loved ones...and of course you.

When was the last time? I let the sun caress my wrinkles. Spoke to Maa and Baboo (even if they are no more there)
Watched the leaves fall…ran and did not think of office at all!

And then it all happened, Brussels, Waterloo, Kukenhoff, Oostende, Namur, Dinant, Luxembourg, Brugge, Paris, Mont Saint Michael, Verona, Trieste, Torino, Florence, Rome, Delhi, Goa, Varanasi, Kolkata...a wanderer on the face of the earth.....

I was expected to be happy...but all I wanted to do was to go and sit in my chair in Tankaila.

I wanted to go home. Five long months and I had forgotten what it felt like to be myself.

I wanted to ogle at the Kanchendzonga, I wanted to touch the cool mist on my skin, I wanted to lose myself in the one single street. I wanted to stand by the window and just breathe.

I wanted to inhale the total shabbiness, and the rains, the pure greediness, the pure indulgence, the pure Kurseong-ness of it all.

I never made it that far.

The wounds of the past months mocked at me from every twist, every turn. Home was not the same again. And yet it was homecoming. Getting back felt like the first breath after nearly drowning. Even if it hurt, it was still Heaven. No matter how depressing, how bleak.

Homecoming is always a return.

Then I heard Baboo calling and it was like I was a child again. No more running to do...it was a beautiful thing to be still, where everyone knows everybody. Be it a trip to the shop below, the man on the road, or the driver driving you up.

Finally the feeling of being myself.

I don't know why, in that rainy afternoon in Trieste, I yearned for family and friends irrevocably…the pain taking enormous proportions. And suddenly Trieste made me want to write. I wanted to sit by the harbour and scribble away. Someday I hope fervently, to be able to come back again, and get lost in its beautiful labyrinths. Trieste is French word for sadness. And above all it so inspired me to write. But one side was the pain of numerous absences, and on the other, much as I wanted to I couldn't take up my pen…I went numb.

I imagine us together in Trieste. We would have walked along, my hand holding your elbow. I don't know but I feel, you would have sung to me. Did Rabindranath ever visit Trieste? You would know. Yes I stood in Trieste on the Bridge…there is something so different in Trieste, from any other place in the world. Trieste is you, charming, romantic and water, which you so adore.

As the heavens poured its love on me, on that cloudy afternoon…the shadows slowly lengthening, I discovered you everywhere, in the dark stone walls of its churches, in the various shades of grey waters, in its narrow meandering paths; Trieste makes me want to dream that one impossible dream…may I?

Sometimes there are wounds that never show on the body, that are deeper and more painful than anything that bleeds. Sigmund Freud didn't much take to the city. I understand that no one commits suicide because they want to die. Then why do they do it? Because they want to stop the pain.

I am glad for once to be back inside the train, on my return from Trieste, but before I leave, I take one last look back at the city of boats and the where the Austrian Hapsburgs no more reside. They too have left like I do leaving other cities…and the tears come gushing down, as I so hate to say goodbye to you, but I promise myself, I will be back again. Suddenly there is sunshine…

The train speeds its way into reality, yet there is hope…and one that fateful day as I left Trieste behind, I had this strange feeling, like I will not only miss the city, but I will miss the person that I was in Trieste…because I will never be the same again.

Our journeys across Europe has changed us forever, because we will never be what we were, when we first started out…and maybe therein lies the hope.

So hand in hand in that rainy evening, we both leave Trieste together, as the newer destinations beckon. The train speeds…in the distance I see the faraway lights pointing to another miracle. You smile that everlasting smile of yours. I put my head on your shoulders. It's home.

"Firenze is magnetic, romantic and busy. Its urban fabric has hardly changed since the Renaissance, its narrow streets evoke a thousand tales, and its food and wine are so wonderful."

- The Lonely Planet

Florence is a culmination of all the Arts. The people of Florence believe that the spirits are imprisoned in the Statues, which adorn this ancient city.

As I stand in the Piazza della Signoria, and look at the statue of Neptune by Ammanati, I hear the legend that he was the mighty river god of the Arno turned into statue because, like Michelangelo, he spurned the love of women. Suddenly I have the urge to be also imprisoned in a statue.

I imagine myself jumping out of a statue, and the look of utter bewilderment on passersby.

Florence is me, intense in its every structure. I hug on to the balustrades of Ponte Vecchio across the River Arno, which is filled with numerous tourists. The city knows from where it comes, but knows not where it goes. As I look across the river, I feel the city is more ancient than it was even supposed to be. The heart of Florence beats in its cobbled pathways and its ancient edifices, its museums brilliant in its contents. The city is a feast for all the five senses, and in all its beauty, it seems to me still alive as it was in the 14th century. Walking across the square, I wonder if I will bump into the creator of my David. Maybe we will discuss pleasantries, and exchange notes, and laugh at our common similarity of thoughts. Such is the charm of Florence. And I always know a charming person.

Visiting Florence is like attending a surprise party every day. Dante Alighieri wrote his first book 'La Vita Nuova' in 14th century Florence. In one of its lanes, I view Dante's home, and I am instantly reminded of the epic poem 'The Divine Comedy.' The Dark poet. I so love everything that is Dark.

Standing in the heart of the city, I ponder. Far away the afternoon sun sinks, behind the cathedral, and the dome turns from coral to burnt aambe-I miss your hand in mine. In the last light of the dusk, Florence comes alive. Resting my tired legs, I want to stretch across the table to hold your hand. As darkness slowly falls over Florence, I want to walk hand in hand with you across the bridge, our shoes rubbing the age old ancient stones. Above the soft silvery moon reflects on your face, as together we watch the dome, lit up now in its tawny wonder, lowered down behind the horizon.

We all breathe in the now, but all our history and even our posterity is already occurring as I walk down the streets of Florence, fading into a jubilant evening light of a day, strangely and even reluctantly, already beginning to end.

'Anyone who has seen Michelangelo's David has no need to see anything else by another sculptor, living or dead.'

- Giorgio Vasini

Does one love a statue? Strange it may sound to you. When I first met him, he came alive to me from my History pages of the great Roman civilization, of the Renaissance, of the great Masters, Michelangelo and Leonardo Da Vinci, of Sandro Botticelli, Andrea Del Verrocchio and Alessandria de Allori. The breathtaking masterpiece of gleaming white marble, which is him.

As I watch the watchful eyes of my David, pulsing veins on the back of the hands, and admire the curve of the taut torso, the flexing of the thigh muscles in the right leg...the absolute perfection of my renaissance masterpiece the Academia Gallery comes alive to me.

It's an uncanny feeling to see him come alive, right in front of one's eyes. I was transported to fifteenth century Florence, to the age of artistry at its zenith.

Over the years, as I grew more and more in love, I learned to appreciate and understand, the Arts, the Music, the Culture, so also the numerous sunsets, and the pulsating rains...as if I was reborn and viewing the world, for the first time ever. The beautiful that so long remained hidden. Taking these first faltering steps, took me to horizons that I had never touched ever, the essay is longer now, then it needs to be, but the answer is safely etched in my soul.

During my visit to Europe, there was just this one person I wanted to meet desperately. It was the harvest of my love. He was David, in his beautiful, ever so familiar, symmetries and intriguing asymmetries; the symmetries and asymmetries, each so very known. Looking at David, I had this knowing feeling that I knew him all along. He is mine, and has always been so. His restful focused eyes, in which I saw my own self reflected. David was inside me.

Time stood suspended at the Academia gallery. I could not touch him, yet I did not need to. I realised I have always caressed those sinews, the taut ravishing torso; I have worshipped him. A sense of deep familiarity. Love occurs in meeting of time with the timeless, the passing moment framed, by what has happened, and what is about to occur. As I leave the gallery, I look at him, for one last time, I don't intend, saying goodbye to my David. My journey in Europe, is coming to a close, in a matter of three days, I will be going back, to where I belong, where I will embrace, my family and friends, sit through all the files in office, look through the photos I have taken, share my little experience, about the cities I have passed through and the people I met along the way. And David will remain, where he is, in my soul. Eternal in his being.

*I*t was a warm evening as we drove down to the Temple of Poseidon. Stravos our Chauffeur spoke nonstop all the way, far away the sun was about to set. There are so many stories about Poseidon. It is believed that King Aegis threw himself into the sea in despair at having sighted the black sail of his son Thesis's ship returning from Crete and his battle with the Minotaur. Theses had previously arranged to show a white sail to indicate his safe return, but he forgot and his father needlessly killed himself...

Latter in the evening...Stavros took us to a beautiful tavern for an amazing Greek meal..." (Friends please travel however near or far...believe me you will not be the same person anymore...I have broken my little savings. I don't care. Life I know will take care of me.)

Paris lies in my imagination like a bridge between, the city of Voltaire of Rousseau, of Liberty, Equality and Fraternity, of Napoléon, a meeting of history and cultures, a background to love…a city where questions stop being asked as much as a place where they begin…and above all it's a city for love, a city for lovers. Someone had once told me never go to Paris without someone you love.

As I stood alone in front of the Eiffel Tower, something inside me had died…like a bare branch against the wind and cold. We could have been together. My body aches, magnifying my pain. I go inside the museum… the paintings and the huge colorful canvases, grips me as does the numerous paintings of bygone centuries, agonised self-portraits. I barely notice the crowds that cluster in front of the pictures. I am suddenly gripped by a little painting. There is something about the grief in the eyes which is similar to mine. This was suffering. I come back again and again to stand in front of the same picture.

I had walked what felt like the whole length of Paris. I walked through the numbered arrondissements, meandering through a food market, grazing at all the famous brands through Champs de Ellyses. I sit on a bench by the side of the Seine, watching the tourists boats go by. I gaze at the moonlight waters and take the Metro through Paris, picking up objects, mentally converting the Euros into Indian Rupees and putting them down again. For me Paris was not a city of Lovers, it was rather a city of Strangers… of strange food, unfamiliar language…

Anyone can get hold of a guide and tick off all the Monuments, but within the very confines of Paris, I wept endlessly for all the poignant emotions that I ever believed in. My paintings of everyone ever loved surpassing the Mona Lisa…

Day two in Sanremo we take in the sea, in all its blue. I can't seem to take my eyes off the Mediterranean. It reminds me of my Geography classes back in school. The thought of being blessed to be in such surroundings hit's me over and over again. Yes I am grateful to you, grateful for all the blessings, grateful for all the good wishes that have been my steady anchor.

Patrizia and me, explore the town together, walk through the beautiful promenade, eat grilled Salmon, in a quaint tavern, and I am reminded of a song, which I can't remember the words, it's about meeting in a tavern...but now I know the feeling. Along with the smell of the sea, I am reminded of the smell of romance.

The best part of being in Sanremo, is the sense of tranquil peace...in the utter simplicity that life has to offer. The ethereal tranquility, and the bread I break and cheese I have, almost makes me feel reincarnated. It's pin drop solitude...and in the distance lies the sea.

Sanremo is an old town dating back to nearly 1297. So deep lies its history. The almost perfectly preserved old town of Sanremo remains exactly as it is. I breathe in the air, the smells of the Mediterranean and feel that life is all and only about, being within. So in my fifty-seventh year on earth, I choose to do things differently. I choose not to bore everyone on Facebook with umpteen photos. I choose to try and go a bit under the table, and stay there all my life if I have a choice. I choose not to look at shops; it does not interest me anymore.

She smiled and said with an enraptured air it sparkles like aquamarine. What does? The moment, it is endless, it hangs in unburdened space like a little aquamarine it is eternal.

*W*e both hit the evening mass on Sunday. Each Church in Europe speaks in own history. I can't stop falling in love with each of the houses of God. Baroque, Gothic, Romanesque architecture stirs my very senses, as does the carvings, the statues, the overhead frescoes, the stained glass windows, the magnificent columns.

My phone camera feels shabby, so insignificant...I almost want to throw it away. It's humbling as I gaze at him, bleeding on the cross, as we each carry ours. Far away the moonlight, watches me light up, as I gather in my arms the inky Italian night.

Back home, dinner is all exotic and excellent. I have never tasted such fare...my taste buds almost want to jump up with joy. I can't stop eating. With every sip and every bite, I savor the extra ordinariness. If only I could frame the same in my tongue forever.

So my destinations have no plans, no exotic names...I love it this way, to take to the cobbled stone ways, as magic unfolds...the markets, the people, the 1922 Restaurant where we stop for pasta, each swirl in my very mind...and I want to give wings to my words so that they reach you...and intoxicate your very senses.
It took me a long time to come into my own
but, now that I am here.
I plan to inhabit me completely....

"*H*ey, you visiting Varanasi!!" the exclamation marks almost jeered at me.

I am a sucker for "happy endings" be it in literature, movies and of course in life too.

My tryst with Bangla Literature is something I am literally ashamed off yet I tried reading a few books enjoyed them, but mostly I read translations, one such book was *"Nowko Dubi"* by Rabindranth Tagore the translation named as "The Wreck" like his numerous other writings, staged often in the backdrop of the ancient city of Varanasi.
A city, whose air I always wanted to breathe. Varanasi, first came alive to me, from the pages of my childhood history books, its numerous *ghats*, it's religious exoticism, it's narrow, cobbled stone alleys, its earthy dusty squalor, a place where history ended, as much as a place where history began. All the more an intense place to stand between death and the very unknown "now."

Varanasi breathes and lives like a real human being, the morning *Surya* hugging the mighty *Ganga*, the incessant *Agni* cleansing the endless dead, miraculously the only place where Death never ends. The majestic evening *Arati* invoking life again.

As I stood intoxicated in its entirety, the three thousand old hallowed city, played havoc into my very blood, the labyrinthine *gallis* caressing my tired feet, the muddy waters of the breath-taking *Ganga* bathing my rusty toes, the gold *zari* of the brilliant *saree* molding my worn old body, the rainbow beads creating a halo around my wrinkled neck, the scented *pan* stirring my nostrils almost into a frenzy.

And like time and again, as it did with many, Varanasi stood carrying my past into my present, and as my feet trudged through the mighty stone steps of the *ghats*, I had this strange feeling of matching my footprints with my forefathers, my glorious heritage, coming passionately alive through my very senses, walking back through the cobbled lanes, realizing that my history and even my future is already occurring as Varanasi almost reluctantly once again 'begins to end.'

*S*aptomi mornings used to be brilliant in Kurseong. Waking up late, to a good scrub and heading towards *Ramkrishna Ashram*, with Maa in toe for the *Aonjoli*...She would insist I fast till the rituals be over, and Baboo would look quite disapprovingly on the whole scenario unfolding.

For me, everything boiled down to Economics and Marx, as I would be dressed in new clothes, new shoes, and a new hand knitted pullover, which I hated wearing, cause it would hide my new dress.

The Ashram premises featured the Incredible India, the solemn priests in their ochre garb, chanting the Devi Mantras, the incense dance, each sense coming alive with the smell and sound of *Pujo*. Mrs P.T Lama, the wife of the Municipal Commissioner, the headmistress of Ramakrishna Mission School, Miss. Shanti Pradhan, the beautiful Mrs. Mayadevi Chettri...familiar faces...the essence of all small towns...everyone resplendent in their beautiful sarees, adorning the almost spartan Ashram.

Durga Pujo in Kurseong was so Pan Indian, with the Nuns from school coming home for a festive lunch. There used to be the annual grand luncheon organised by my parents for all their official colleagues. Irrespective of origins, everyone attended. School friends would be sharing *Pujo* space, gulping traditional Bengali sweetmeats like bitter tablets (we all preferred the *Alu Dum* and *Sailroti* which would soon follow with *Dasain*, lacking the Bengali sweet tooth)

So finally the *Anjoli* would end...the priest would sprinkle holy water from the Ganga...purifying us of all our negativity...and the chilly autumn morning of Kurseong would reverberate with the chant of *"Om shanti! Om shanti! Om shanti"*...the voice echoing and re-echoing across the mighty Himalayas. Love you all.

Children write essays in school about the unhappy, tragic, doomed life to Anna Karenina. But was Anna really unhappy she chose passion and paid for her passion– that's happiness. She was a free, proud human being.

- Aleksandr Solzhenitsyn, Cancer Ward.

*I*t's been crazy all these past few days, with my aches and pains suddenly turning ballistic and taking center stage. I mean there was poor me left with nothing but clutching on to medicines and my poor bones. Osteoarthritis was pushing me in a dark dead alley. I couldn't wash my face, (I still have my bath like my forefathers did…not used to showers) and in this stifling heat I just couldn't lift a mug of water, and instead of water dripping it was tears. Mundane things that I did everyday were getting painful, like watering my little plants, turning a door knob, lifting a jug, wearing my garments. My darling friends took in all my tantrums as I went cry baby like in Kindergarten, and every message, every word, every call, of theirs made me feel all the more vulnerable.

Well, yesterday night after ages I stumbled upon some freaking luck. With Nikkon away in Kurseong and Babua away at his workplace, I was ponderously alone. My aches and pains too felt a lot calmer. Then came a beautiful message from a dear soul, who suggested that I stay back home, and soothe my aches with some good music. "Hey Jude don't make it bad take a sad song and make it better." The Beatles were perfect company.

Saturday morning, dawned bright. I woke up late and brewed myself a cup of the perfect Anandini tea and relished each and every droplet. Started a conversation, with Basanti on missing Nikkon and read some hand written poems [handwriting is sheer luxury these days] from a favorite diary. Solitude had never ever been so personal. I carried heaven on my back throughout the day. Far away the sun met the horizon, love shows its greatest magnificence at the time of leaving I guess.

*A*s Devi Durga slayed the notorious pair *Chando* and *Munda,* on the eve of *Nobomi,* I destroyed all my demons of the past few months. It had rained here in Siliguri as *Sandhikhan* engulfed twenty-four minutes before *Asthami,* and the first twenty-four minutes of *Nobomi.* Bucephil and me had stepped out on the streets to get a heady a whiff of the rain soaked earth. *Pujo* always transports me home to Kurseong to that magical moment of 'starry starry nights,' of the winter line, of the evening chilly breeze, a promise of fiery orange skies as the sun hid behind the clouds racing against the mighty Himalayas. Miss the Himalayas! Sudden flashes like these makes you yearn even more to return to where one's heart belongs. I recollect my Father mentioning how significant it was to make one's final offerings to Maa *Durga,* on *Nobomi* eve. Trudging with friends uphill to Eagle's Craig, on *Sandhikhan,* would always be magical. Far below the chants of the Priest, would cut across the stillness of the hills...in the distance the lights of Siliguri would beckon like the hundred and eight earthen oil lamps, twinkling in the dusk, matching the hundred and eight stars, above likewise the *Sandhi Pujo* lotus offerings.

Back home during *Sandhikhan,* the enchantment would perfume the air. The oil lamps, the autumnal dusk, Maa, adorned in marigolds, the faraway chants... commemorating the victory of good over evil. As the night approaches...the moment standing atop Eagle's Craig, lingers through my memory...tiny yet brave...

*I*t's early morning in Puri...the season of *basonto*? When colours run riot hugging mother earth, a lazy stroll, and my eyes come upon the *bogunvilla.*

Across miles our heartbeats make breath catching adjustments, as the other partakes in the festivities of *"dol"* with friends and families. Travelling with loved ones has been a long-lost dream… abandoned, and buried in the sands of time.
Puri was drizzly, gloomy absolutely perfect for me. I tried the most wonderful seafood, stayed in the most amazing boutique hotel, and wandered through the beaches, experiencing the shells and sands of each. At first I could not come to terms about travelling alone. Travelling together had become a habit. Then something shifted, a plane ticket, the first step towards adjustments. Travelling solo gave me wings, it gave me words...wherever I went a little piece of heart followed me on...my backpack seemed a little more heavier than usual.

I scan across the rocks in Jabalpur, as far as my eyes can see. At a distance is Gir. It hits me this Geography, the business of miles. I weave my own tales, of bumping into others at airports. I wonder if we all will look the other way...and then impermanence whispers…"Hey you, how can you abandon me? Someday maybe I will again join your paths."

Destined by fate, someday maybe we will all get it all right.

"I awaited so long
to touch your face
Without my eyes
for years I did not understand
my glances were caresses."
Rumi

*W*hen the mist cleared, I could see silvery clouds on which tall Angels might stand. No cute little Christmas Angels, but high stern Angels like the Nuns back in school, whose faces were sad and serious from being near God all day and hearing his decisions about the world. (Sorry for the gender bias, in assuming God is a male) And so I headed home through beautiful Rohini as the fog above Dowhill swirled down gently in a greyish haze beyond the window at 'home'. Kurseong felt like a dream.

In Didi's *"aahgan"* the age old bornfire is brightly lit, and the twigs crackle with orange and crimson sparks, as the night air is perfumed with the smell of burnt tea. The dry embers lit our faces. We have gathered here after years, to cherish our memories and forge ahead with our bonds.

Steaming mugs of warm tea pass hands. Tankaila is home free. After years we are all up home. The best part of losing Maa and Baboo is finding a place to store their thoughts, their memories, their feelings far away in the night sky above Eagle's Craig I look at the fading stars, still faintly visible, and wonder if they are up there? Have they managed to survive in space? Have people managed to stay alive there for hundreds of years? Getting answers to my questions is unlikely. And then I look at everyone around me. I get my answers. Yes, we have all survived and confidently sorted our lives, to gather again for Christmas biting on a piece of the age old plump cake, and I know what I really want for Christmas. I want my childhood back. Nobody is going to give me that. I don't know whether it makes sense anyway. It is about the child of now. You and me. Waiting behind the door of our hearts for something wonderful to happen.

Merry Christmas!

Poush Parbon, would always be a grand affair at Jakhirpur. Early morning as the dew settled down on the blades of grass, and the sun played peek a boo on the pillars of our ancestral home, the domestic help would be busy, wiping the courtyard with cow dung and water, for the festivities.

The stone floors of our house would be polished to perfection for Thamma's intricate *Alpana*...not one motif inaccurate, each more splendid than the other.

The white paste of rice flour and water would be my favourite. The huge home would be covered with *Alpana* each more beautiful than the other. I would go about my way, my tiny fingers dipping the cotton into the white coloured paste as I ventured shyly into the world of motifs and my first brush with drawings. So pretty would be Thamma's *Alpana*, that many from the village would come to view it all.

On each motif, one would place grains of rice, *durba* and *sindur* the white of the motif hugging the green yellow and red. It was to be my first foray into the World of Art.

Huge amount of *"pithays"* would be made to feed the cows and the bullocks and buffaloes. They would also wear *sindur* and a design would be made on each of their foreheads. They would all look so pretty.

Today my son barely knows what *pithay* is. I go to designer shops and buy a few of these sweetmeats, and celebrate the occasion.

So I laud you all my dear friends who have made an attempt to uphold what I understand is meant by traditions. Traditions define us, let's try and keep it alive. Just for one day let KFCs and Domino's take a backseat.

"Tradition is a guide and not a jailer. "

- M. Somerset Maugham

In Reverence of one's Ancestors.

*M*ake friends with mediocrity, it's the place of balance.

As a child, growing up in Kurseong, *Mahalaya*, was like any school going normal day. Yet, with unbridled anticipation one woke up to the early morning chants, by the *Late Briendra Krishna Bhadra,* that heralded the coming of *Pujo.* The crispy autumn dawn would echo, and re-echo with the deep baritone, of *Birendra Krishna* as one cuddled close to Maa and Baboo, ears glued to the transistor. I didn't understand anything, nor did I even try to, but like all our generations, our parents in their own beautiful way, tried to imbibe into us a sense of culture, a sense of our splendid heritage.

Today, for my son, *Mahalaya* is a day to wake up late, relax...a welcome break in the middle of a week of work.Getting up early morn! I must be stark mad even to remotely suggest.

With the passing of years *Birendra Krishna Bhadra* has become passé, so has the transistor ...the new generation *Mahalaya* is sleek TV shows watched or not watched on huge screens, a cruise on the *Ganga* and so on and so forth...

Sometimes I wonder, do most of us in our generation think alike? Do we miss and try and uphold traditions in their traditional best or is it a makeover of *Mahalaya* that excites us more...

So like every other year I tread to a river nearby, sit beside it and meditate on the souls of my ancestors, clinging on to maybe a single drop of culture lost. Holding on to a memory gone.... offering my invocation in deep gratitude to them, without whom

I would have had no name, without whom I would have had no
existence.

Ya Devi Sarbabhuteshu
Vishnu Mayati Sharpita
Namastasyai Namastasyai Namastasyai Namo Namaha

The book *"Freedom at midnight"* written by Dominique Lapierre and Larry Collins, had been a rage during my college days. In a narrative from the book, on India's partition, the authors mentioned that, to the excitement and thrill of Sardar Patel, the then interior Minister of the domain of India, a deal had been proposed to the Viceroy. Patel had told the Viceroy "It's got to be everybody. If you can bring me a basket filled with every apple off the tree. I will buy it." Larry Collins and Dominique Lapierre wrote, "The last Viceroy of India and India's future Minister of States bargained like carpet merchants over the States." However, Kashmir was not an easy apple, to fall in the basket that Mountbatten had promised to Sardar Patel. But Nehru was adamant...he wanted the Kashmiri apple at any cost...

Since months, changing miserably again into a year, the BSNL service provider on my mobile had been deteriorating, almost dying. Contacting me was getting to be difficult and exasperating. Complaints of me being constantly 'unreachable' and thereby 'unresponsive,' was getting static. Meanwhile everyone was taking to the Jio, and praises of it being the best service provider was one constant tune that kept humming in my ears, like an irritant bumble bee.

But similar to the Kashmiri apple, I adamantly played loyalty games, with my BSNL. The sim card had been in my possession since the inception of my journey with handsets, a journey spanning more than twenty 'odd' or should I say 'even' years. It was a kind of a blind faith to be a part of Government of my Country, bordering on a patriotic culture that did not want to go in for "private" service providers so on and so forth...and come what may I had whatsoever no intentions of falling into the Ambani band wagon (no offence meant please.) But then, likewise to the fate of the Kashmiri apple, and connectivity through BSNL reaching an all time low. I finally, accepted defeat,

as I gave up my long lost fight and resorted to picking up a Jio
sim card for my phone.

As I write this, I understand BSNL employees have not received their salaries this month...and the fate of many Government undertakings are on the chopping board....

I was speeding back in a Kolkata cab, one of those broken down, splintered yellow Ambassador cabs, which had seen better days. It was a frenzied Indian afternoon, when the cab stopped at one of those innumerable, overcrowded, chaotic traffic junctions that the city thrives on. As the taxi crawled its way through the maze, I noticed a small child; barely six year's old selling balloons. He kept pleading "Aunty they are just ten rupees each please could you buy one?" I looked at the scrawny skinny minor citizen of my country, and something momentous tugged at my heart. I was hitting a new year carrying with me the blood stains of hundreds of mangled children, ailing and hungry kids, the absolute death of humanity. How do we go about our useless and meaningless lives, knowing that we too are guilty and culpable. I take out some little currency, hand it over to a child whose country had won a Noble Peace prize the very year for standing up for child labour. How does it feel to live in a world where we choose one's highest right and not one's darkest wrong, where we lift each other instead of always and forever putting each other down?

I promised myself on the threshold of the New Year that I would try to make a tiny effort to rebuild my soul and so the two balloons stand illuminating my tiny abode. Happiness for all of you out there, for the New Year.

"Journeys to relieve your past?" was the Khan's question at this point, a question which could also have been formulated: Journeys to recover your future?" And Marco's answer was: Elsewhere is a negative mirror. The traveler recognises little that is his, discovering the much he has not had and will never have."

Italo Calvino, Invisible Cities.

During the long vacations I did nothing, except make a journey home. Many questioned whether I had any plans of going elsewhere. "No" was my answer. I just needed to go home. To relive my past, to unite with the present and to hope for a future of clarity rather than certainty. In my everyday classes of nothingness that I attended, I reconnected and discovered much. The fragrance of a soul who said I taught her to smell roses and dark coffee. The chemistry of her words rippled joys through my veins. Home really smelt good. I wanted more and more and hungrily I gorged on Frida Kalho's Diary...gifted by another soul. Kalho writes "Diego, I'd like to paint you, but there are no colours, because there are so many, in my confusion, the tangible form of my great love."

So in my nothingness comes Facebook with friendship anniversaries and I stumble upon words that I want to archive. A soul echoes on what we share. "What can I say like stumbling on an uncut diamond"...In reply I want to say so much, yet I land up saying nothing" and I want to add I am blessed to be alive in your friendship.

Through the journey of my nothingness I achieve *Moksha* through every day gems, and there it is…"and drinking water to celebrate the end of a meal, I become aware, again, that grace is the only style that matters." Her writings always border on serious discourses and I am afraid to say anything...yet I reflect on that one word she used "grace" as I surge through the pages of nothingness.

And so in all my nothingness I unknot and dismantle more...a soul reflects on sleeping below the stars, I mention, why don't you post some more of those pictures...she says she wants to "detox from technology"...I feel her freedom in my blood. I respond to life, all over again.

So here I am constantly wondering as all of you spread your fragrances, in my life, as you tell me "nothing can beat friendship" and the best part is none of you have ever looked at it that way...It has been your nature to be like that.

Friendship is heady...its my home, your home, blissful silence, memories of another day, Jean Paul Satre, Homer and the Odysseus, sunsets to live for, Italian Wine, the dusty furniture, faded cushions, steaming momos, homemade cakes, damp blankets…Yes, friendship is everything I need, I can go on and on.

*D*o I envy those people whose lives always add up to four?

Always perfect!

These are long months…

when life comes out misshapen

and every memory seems remote and untouched…

I yearn incessantly like a fever-gripped for those days of endless rain across the hills, when everything felt so safe and familiar, (not the mathematical kind) the spicy aroma from the kitchen, of *kidchuri,* and Baboo, being home after a hard day's work, as I draw faces on the misty glass panes and write my name…a hundred times.

Today, I have the luxury of not heading to work…yes, not another two adding up to another two.

I sit scanning diligently through the umpteen WhatsApp posts which has every philosophy to make my day and life better…One particular post catches my eye which says…"Everything we hear is an opinion and not a fact, and everything we see is a perspective and not a truth…" I ponder, as I 'hear' Bucephil barking and Nikkon mouthing 'bye' before he leaves for work…I wonder if the words we use in love or when we hurt…measures up to an opinion.

Whether missing going home is a perspective and not the truth?…I also try to understand "What if love was just a perspective?"

"I can't emphasis enough the power of support."

- Joshi Perry

The humidity in Kolkata, takes a backseat as one enters the sprawling campus of the Tata Medical Center. It almost feels surreal, amongst the welcoming greens, riot of flowers, huge open spaces, and yet somewhere in between it all, lies struggling hopes, scarred joys, some little pain and yes immense gratitude.

As survivors, one shares a commonality a kind of mute assurance, as one relates to one's own experiences. So much similitude it almost feels family...and everyone, and everyone talks of hope. By now some faces wear a cloak of recognition, of strange bondings, the lady in the wheelchair; the tall bald girl; the ever smiling youth. I am grateful I don't meet children.

Most days, there is no song in my heart, yet I sing, smile at the Hospital staffs, thank them for all helps received, say 'hello!' to a survivor. I see a young girl sporting a T shirt "no hair don't care." I guess without hair, a queen is still a queen...I so want to tell her this. At times I want to hug each and every survivor, and tell them, I need to hug each one of you, to truly appreciate, what it means to be alive, to be able to touch, to be able to breathe and feel.

Cheers to each soul, as they do an awesome job of not dying.

I wake up to a blamy cloudy monsoon morning, just my type of weather, and there is so much I need to do, but all I want to do, is lie in bed with Bucephil and write…soak in the raindrops of my own words.

These are long months…and every memory sounds like a long lost note…which is to say I don't know the difference between haunting and hanging on…these days of endless torrents across my hearth and heart…seeking to celebrate as well as mourn the incessant droplets. I am both assertive and aggressive about my passions, at times I considered horrific, like bunking office to watch the play of clouds, or drinking red wine in a perfect crystal wine glass with *maachayer jhol* and *mistis*. Frankly, women around the world still struggle with the glass ceilings and boxes they aren't allowed to cross or tick off.

Sometimes my own dramas haunt me, yet they lack melodrama… I am simply sad and pure…I feel things clearly, unclouded by malice or social stigma…like Bucephil's version of the world… animals are good, the earth needs love. So let me grow plants in my miniature veranda, eat *mistis*…and when I love I do it with infinite generosity. Travel and love, love love…and wear flowers in my hair (I learnt that from Rebs, and from my favourite icon Frida Kahlo.)

I want to love the earth and anything which is earthy…at times I am full of pains, both physical and beyond…most days I can't drape a saree or put a belt in the loops of my jeans, or open a tap or anything which is tight, my fingers lack strength…but, today I am ecstatic…the monsoons have finally come to my home, and I make a remarkable discovery as I read Hayden Herrera's biography on Frida Kahlo where Hayden describes that Frida had addressed many love letters not to her famous husband Diego Rivera but to her lover Josè Bartoli. Hayden Herrera describes these previously unpublished letters to "my Bartoli" as steamy with unbridled sensuality and…like Kalho's paintings, extraordinary direct and physical.

The long distance passionate relationship is best depicted in the letters that the two lovers exchanged during the 1940s. The letters express the admiration and adoration that the two artists had for one another, while their thoughts and feelings are detailed in hundred pages of correspondences. In one of her letters, Kahlo wishes for a child with Bartoli…"If I was not in the condition I am in now, and if it were a reality, nothing in my life would give me more joy. Can you imagine a little Bartoli or a Mara." Mara was how Kahlo used to sign off her letters. A nickname Bartoli gave her. I can't stop reading her outpourings of emotions and sensuous passion…and the rains continue unabated as I pour through pages and pages of the proof of Kahlo's love.

It's late evening. Outside, the rains synchronise with my soul, the mobile stands mute, I scan through the call logs, nothing interests me, I look out of the window and stretch my hands to feel the drops of rain caressing my arthritic worn, deformed and frail fingers…as I finally learn to grasp how Bartoli's love must have strengthened Kahlo, ever so much, and gave her hope for a long and happy life full of unquenchable passion…meanwhile the downpour persist…ever so incessantly, eagerly and frenzied.

*A*n early morning Purchase Committee Meeting with the Vice Chancellor and you have no clue. A friend casually talks you into believing something and you can see right through all the fake. A video shared by a friend on your WhatsApp and she says she identifies it with you. Another video comes along which makes you go all nostalgic and you know you "have a friend." Crooning Columbus alike as you discover new music on YouTube. The smell of office tea. Great ideas in the middle of the meeting. A new movie, a new book. Old movies old books.

A phone call from home, suggesting a weekend.

Gateway, once again to the *Ganga*, but at a different destination… Songs that get you. Friends who get you. Plane journeys on the schedule. Sunsets shared with Bucephil on an evening walk.

*T*he DSLR which you had gifted lies in a corner of the storewell. I seem not to be able to use it anymore, much as I would want to. Over the months, my hand has been slowly giving away. Doing ordinary things as simple as opening a sealed bottle of packaged water or opening a flash door, gets harrowingly difficult. Lugging a DSLR, is something which I have stashed away, in the backyards of my perceptions…at airports, in offices everywhere I reach out to people for everyday help for doing ordinary mundane things…and as the five years culminate I question myself…how long am I going to live? And as time keeps absconding, I realise I have so much more to give.

Someone had once mentioned, express your love as often as you can, to all those whom you dearly love, for you will never know when will be the last time you can say it at all…five years, and the memories still knock the wind out of me…and yes I so want to make so much more of them, so what if my hand does not function properly, so what if I get as busy as a maniac, so what… I never want to put a band-aid over my shortcomings, and sit in the confines of any 'air-conditioned comfort zone…'

I want to desperately lug on to that DSLR…and move on…as you say to give one's hundred percent, and not to pick and choose to whom or to what I am giving to…with each passing day, I want to breathe more, love even more, and ignore the clock, and put my friend, destiny, at the back seat, of the car… Rather, I want to say "Hello life!"…maybe it might be for the one last time I would be saying it…

It is easy to be responsible, to be able to love those near you and closest to you, what is far more difficult is to love, fellow human beings, with all their imperfections and defects…to give them equally and if required even more…five years is a long time in one's life. Today, I have matured enough to understand that I would not have loved, if there was something not lacking within me…but the discovery of a similar lack within another offends oneself…at the midlife, I no more seek any answers…if I have to seek answers all I would find would be duplicates of my own problems.

So many beautiful years, and yes I have learned to finally relish pain in all its dimensions and understand that all the broken pieces within me are coming together to form a whole, so what if it is a blemished and a scarred whole.

I will call down the stars each night,

bid them stray from their lofty posts,

to kiss each one in gratitude

for giving me something

which I wanted most.

Gao Xingjian, winner of the Nobel Prize for Literature had titled his book *"Soul Mountain"*…it's mid afternoon on a misty rain-drenched Saturday, while I go through Gao's writing…at my "Soul Home"…as Tankaila embraces me with all her love affection and blissful solitude…

Strangely I don't miss anyone, except those who are no more and yes my darling Bucephil. Tankaila is not for the glamorous, neither is it for the ones, who are accustomed to bright lights luxury and those whose lives always add up to a perfect four… the single malts, the designer clothes, the perfect conversations… do I sound a wee bit like the 'grapes are sour kind types…so what if I do! It does not bother me…' Tankaila is for the weak hearted, the broken, the outcast and the insider.

I wander endlessly from room to room…I recall much; the day my ears were pierced, lying in the open terrace on an August evening, and counting the stars…the *Bijoya Dashami* get together and yes I remember Chinky. I am aware that at this moment I am surrounded by a world of people who are gone. I want to sit with Maa and Baboo again, at the dining table and listen to them chatting about trifling things. I want to hear their voices to see their eyes…I don't want to see you, I don't want to hear your voice. I know Maa and Baboo are worried for me, of the way I am living my life, my health… they understand I can't go on like this…sounds strange again, the dead worrying about the living…

The mists, over powers my vision, as I search for my childhood…there is no aroma from the kitchen…no green moss on the walls, no fresh flowers in the vases, no elongated moon atop Dowhill…instead, there is the shrill ring of the phones…that cuts across the comfort of my aloneness. I don't want to deserve anyone's voice…I just want the luxury of myself…a pure and fragrant concoction that shall intoxicate my very being. The more people forbid doing something, the more I want to do it, like drift here and there without leaving traces. There are so many places in this world, and so many places to visit, but apart from Tankaila there is nowhere for me to put down my roots, to have a simple refuge, to live a simple life. It makes me wonder how people survive away from their roots.

I realise, much as I want to there is little I can seek in this world, so there is no need to be greedy…greedy for a presence, greedy for a voice…the months and years preceding this obsession to be greedy had robbed me of enjoying my stillness…cause at the end everything is just gone, and what I will achieve are just memories: 'hazy intangible dream like memories'…Tankaila grows on me as a memory.

I met her in the crossroads, a woman wearing a veil of pain on her face. We greeted one another, and I said to her, "Come to my abode and be my guest."

And she came. She sat with me, accounted chronicles of betrayal, of lies, and tales of love songs sung by men to every woman.

And then she looked around my hearth, and gazed at the simple beauty of the flowers on the veranda, the adoration of my dog, the simple wonders of my family.

And all her stories that were born out of bitterness of the days faded in the summer-like light of the dusk.

"The present we are impulsive, goverened in large part by emotions and immediate desire."

- Abhjit . V. Banerjee

Poor Economics: rethinking poverty & the ways to mend it.

Love and Economics- can these two be entitled "Das Kapital Revisited."

In 1990 when I first decided I desperately needed to have some semblance on four wheels...Karan Johar was my banker then...*Dilwale Dulhania Le Jaingay*...had hit the Indian market, and hubby dear's sensex was hand in hand with Mr. Khan...it was the honeymoon period...I didn't even have to look adoringly. The car was at my doorstep. First car like first love...well! well!

Come September, the year was 2005. I had shifted base from the premises of the sprawling residential quarters of North Bengal University to Siliguri and needed a car to ferry me to work and home regularly. I restarted gazing adoringly at hubby dear once again. Prayed to Karl Marx more fervently but then Economics refused to see eye to eye with me. My dwindling Bank balance was proof enough that what Karan Johar was churning on screen was all trash. So the next step was to join the Women's Commission, where all I wanted was gender equality, only on matters of Economics though!

2009...dawned...and practically every morning I was waking up from the wrong side of the bed. Meanwhile the four wheels of mine, fervently cried out for retirement benefits. By then Economics had enough and had decided to divorce me once and for all. And finally for the third time, I shifted my dwindling gears of my four wheels and strived towards Parental Empowerment. Genetic Economics...Huh!

2015, the little four wheels by now literally looking like peeled onion. Once again I needed to function...and as Karl Marx turned on his music...I wondered what was the music that I should listen to? *"Jodi tor dak shunay keu na aashey tobey ekla cholo ray?"*

That's exactly what I am doing, so what if there are no likes for 'poor economics anymore.' No parental empowerment too forthcoming. Today as I get back from office, the new four wheels once again remind me. Economics is all about beating your own drum. What say, Sanchari?

"And that's it."

- Trista Mateer

One remembers the month of August all too vividly.

It was hard to be the one who left, as it was to be the one who stayed. People always talked about being left behind, but nobody talks about how difficult it was to pack up. It always felt like you were digging for a reason not to open up the front door. Every time one left, it got harder to walk back in. **One day one won't be able to anymore…**

In total, one must have undertaken at least seven to eight trips, it was not easy, being a frequent flyer, and Airports had become as familiar as the Vice Chancellor's Chamber.

The year one did things one had never done before…travelled to Nepal, to Bhutan and to half of Europe. Every place one went to was unapologetic, sighing. At times one stood bereft in Airport lounges and kept reaching out…from the snowcapped peaks of Machhapucharay to the tulip gardens of Kukenhoff, and from your favorite chair at Tankaila…for oneself every journey began with a 'No' and for you every journey ended with a reason.

The year saw one's 'proper responses' maturing into a 'no' response. For one a proper response was immediately reacting, fighting, crying, not taking a call and writing a different kind of poem. Instead now one drinks a glass of water, stares at the name on the phone and explains to oneself that for many years every day one had dialed to each other, and shall do so for the rest of one's lives.

In the year one did away with all the old intense melodramatic love poems, and concentrated more on quality write-ups. In the year that followed, one was pampered with diamonds and Economics became one's favorite subject…while Music and Literature went for a toss.

But whatever in the year that followed one became more confident in love. One panicked a lot less, hardly got insecure and it had all been about finding a new beginning. The "I" had taken a radical shift to the 'us'…and the comfort zone seemed to exist with some degree of force.

Well, one comes into this world of births and deaths. No one will die for one, nor one for anyone.

How wonderful to die for someone, how wonderful to live for someone…

"The first quarter-century of your life was done better lived under the cloud of being too young for things, while the last quarter century would normally be shadowed by the still darker cloud of being too old for them; and between these two clouds, what small and narrow sunlight illumines a human lifetime!"

- James Hilton, Cost Horizon

Sandup, the Tibetan Mastiff's bark, sliced through the stillness of the dense night air, as I gazed far into the vivid darkness.

Much below, the lights in the valley of Paro, sparkled like a bevy of stars. Deep in the mountain I rested, in the lap of Tara, the feminine concept that encircles the Buddha.

Plus fifty, is a dangerous age as you embrace your wrinkles, your aches and pains, of not only the physical, but also the mind. So I embarked on this search, for a spirituality that sought the tranquil solitude and maybe a madness of another type. As the journey mellowed into sunset, the detoxification of the body and soul couldn't be made more glorious. And the road soaked in knowledge, hugged my very being healing and breathtakingly ordinary.

So I cradled myself, and let go of hearth and work, for a two day Retreat in a far off remote monastery, in the heart of the Dragon Kingdom, in search of the unknown, and trying desperately to find some semblance of a comfort zone with the numerous questions that battered me.

It was overwhelming, befriending oneself, deep in the beautiful Valley absolutely remote and basic, as my emotions and spirits sought to encounter the 'Ultimate.'

"It is never to late to ask yourself 'Am I ready to change myself?' However old we are, whatever we went through, it is always possible to be reborn. If each day is a copy of the last one, what a pity! Every breath is a chance to reborn. But to reborn into a new life you have to die before dying."

- Shams Tabrizi

In 2017, friendships helped me to see myself in another's eyes and I realised all friendships of any length are based on continued mutual forgiveness. Without mercy and tolerance all friendships die. I made so many new friends in 2017, and much as I hugged on to my 'aloneness' I also realised that any journey is impossible to accomplish alone so along I trudged with my friends, believed in them, and sparkled in their aura.

In 2017, I drank mountains through the Alps on a train journey, forged streams in Brugge, smelled the flowers at Kukenhoff, soaked the sun in at Candolim, splashed in the rain, back home, walked the beaches in Oostende, cried for love on the banks of the Seinne, cleansed my soul in the muddy waters of Varanasi and yes hugged on to the trees at Rydak with all my vulnerabilities, while Rome stood, a silent testament to it all, in the middle of that warm May afternoon.

As 2017 slowly moves towards its sunset. I stand all by myself in this new found intimacy, as I shed my outer skin. I realise the best moments this year has been, laying on bed, with Bucephil, sleeping ever so peacefully at my feet, music soothing my ears and I know exactly how Keats must have felt when he wrote his "Ode to a Nightingale."
"My heart aches, and a drowsy numbness pains
My sense, as though of hemlock I had drunk."

Note bene, KM my Acharya, I breathe you. Gratitudes for everything.

"How could you give me life, and take from me all the inappreciable things that raise it from the state of conscious death?"

- Charles Dickens, Hard Times

The temperature on the Smartphone indicates 16° Celsius. I smuggle all the more inside the synthetic blanket and long for those soft red quilts which had been so much a part of growing up days as the cold wintry breeze does strange things to my senses.

Kurseong December 1973

Winter in Kurseong was not just a season; it was much more than that. It was wearing a Navy Blue overcoat to school, tucking one's icy cold fingers inside one's pockets, the stockings one wore, thick hand knitted woolen socks, mittens with the tips of the fingers cut off in such a way so as to enable one to write and turn pages. Collecting twigs from the pruned tea bushes for evening bonfires, the night air perfuming itself with the incense of burnt tea, the azure winter line...and the equally long shadows atop the Mirik hills. Endless readings late into the night, as the overhead lamp cast its eerie shadows on the whitewashed walls. In fact most of my early readings in life were completed during the long winter months.

A whole new world of Dicken's and Hardy and O'Henry, the Legends of Greece and Rome, of the Odyssey and the Iliad, of Snowhite and Red Riding Hood, of Mills and Boons and Sarat Chandra and translations from Rabindranath, evenings with Somerset Maugham Jane Austen. Robinson Crusoe and Gulliver's Travels, and yes Little Women, as I wondered dreamlike, with Alice. The oranges were the sweetest that I have ever tasted, so were the Swiss Buns and fruit cakes that came from the local bakery, all complete with red cheeks and an equally red running nose, above all not a care in the world!!

Darjeeling December 1983

"Do you hear what I am saying?
Is it misty inside my dream for you?"
Benny's coffee, tucking my hands in his pocket after a movie on the way back to the hostel. Endless waits at the college canteen for the sun to make an appearance. The fabulous Tibetan wool pullovers. Getting into bed with jeans on, so that one didn't have to change early morning for breakfast. Far away only the Kanchendzonga stood witness.

December 2013 Siliguri.

Electric Blankets, Chinese Heaters, Thermals from Marks and Spencers, Green Tea Bags, Creams Body Lotions Lip Balms, Online shopping for Winter Wear, Designer cakes. Welcome to the lifeless, plastic monosyllabic 21st century! I wish I could take a winter holiday and search for my lost soul.

Woke up early like I abnormally do and went to the gym. For once my shoes were not unpatriotic, as I touched base on the treadmill with sneakers on instead of bedroom slippers (I was shown the door last time) and an old Tee which sort of hid my oodles of fat.

The day backtracked with fun filled lethargy and long moony conversations on Graham's Bell leaving me hungry enough to gobble loads of sinful lunch instead of the usual fare of stale office bread.

Well! well the new thing in town is indeed sharing holidays on the phone.

"Hi! How is Simla?"

"How is Siliguri?" so on and so forth and soon I was swimming in the warm waters of Varkala Beach and sipping roadside *chai* in Amritsar. WhatsApp pictures, messages, sound bytes of waves and birds crooning. Disturbed bliss!

By the middle of the evening, I needed to have a long overdue date with the bathing room ("I am a room too she moaned." Getting jealous of the bedroom huh?) so, I laid down ever so comfortably on the bed so that the feeling would pass…as I tried to eat the clock.

Time consuming right!

And so the day marched on. I meditated and realised the ultimate truth that the first fifty years of your childhood are always the most beautiful. Kind of weird! But truth no doubt.

And now it's almost time for bed, so I guess I will just check my email, WhatsApp, Instagram, Facebook and one full session of Trump and Clinton.

So, I say no to 'real' people and a lot of yes and yes to my 'virtual' friends. "Help!" I retort back. Before you all resort to the option 'block.'

'After my father left,
Part of me became
Determined
To always do the leaving'

Honeybee,
Trista Mateer

Years back, you had spoken of a 'final destination.' Among all the European town or cities that I had the good fortune to visit, Rome to me marks the end and also the resurrection of a journey. During the course of my travels, Rome, to me stands as the most beautiful of all the horizons.

Guess I didn't make this journey in order to find the words missing from my life, yet I missed family and home irrevocably, and realised how magical my little world was. I went in search of a universe, and what did I get…a magical 'biverse' surrounded by my very soul.

Yes, I understand, I could have also, reached the same conclusions, without ever leaving my little bedroom, but sometimes you have to travel a long way, in order to find what is near. I needed to celebrate my courage. We all set off in search of the unknown. I was sad for a while, maybe I even wept, yet by the end of it all, I have found what I have been looking for in my entire life. I thank my Buddha for giving me the unique experience, of having travelled to so many places. Yes, life is indeed a journey. We carry on meeting, and again saying goodbye for all eternity. A departure followed by a return, and a return followed by a departure.

I did not want to say goodbye to Rome, like never ever wanting to say goodbye to you all. Permanence is such a dreadful thing. As I left Rome that fateful afternoon I told her, I will be seeing her again someday, and I made it sound like a promise. And I want to never ever make promises I don't want to keep.

Throughout my travels, I carried you all on the insides of me, in my rib cage. My heart was like a suitcase, lugging you all around from one destination to another. At times, it broke my back; I was bleeding, yet for even once I never left you. And I shall always carry you all on the insides of me.

So as I look at Rome from my flight window, I like to think, that one day I will both be old enough, to find novelty in childish things again. I will lay down our keys, and pick myself like a stubborn lock, that won't open ever for anyone else…never again.
The Final Destination.

ACKNOWLEDGEMENT

I render my deepest gratitude to each and every one of you dear Helenites for your constant encouragement in believing in me. Without you all, this book would have never seen a dawn. Heartfelt appreciation to the rest of all my friends who have been my journey mates, over the years, it was your dignified capacity for friendship, that helped me weave words with my emotions.

Gratitudes to my Publishers at Woven Words for their patience in working with my editing and contributing enormously towards the conceptualization of the book. The results are there for you to visualize.

Gratitudes in abundance for the kindness of my Office Staff, for working tirelessly beyond your work hours, to help bring my words to print.

To my family for believing in me, egging me on and lovingly supporting my passions. Amongst them I only take your name Bucephil.

In Memory of Baboo, Maa, Bunu and Thamma whose clear Souls have been love and blessings. I miss you .